How to Cope with Loneliness after the Loss of a Friend or Your Spouse of Many Years

Volume 3

Kenneth E. Murrey, Sr.

ISBN 979-8-88851-280-7 (Paperback)
ISBN 979-8-88851-281-4 (Digital)

Covenant Books
11661 Hwy 707
Murrells Inlet, SC 29576
www.covenantbooks.com

Readers, loneliness is a dark place of its own in time.
You sleep with it, you eat, and walk with it.
Just when you think you are okay, there it is.
Suddenly, without warning, there is loneliness. It is now part
Of your life. People say to you, it will get better in time.
No, it will not. Loneliness is like time;
It will always be there, and you will still be lonely.
I had sixty years of true love, no time nor talking to anyone
Can give that back to me.
Loneliness can be like sudden death. If you can't cope at some
Point with it, time is not on your side, but loneliness will
Always be there. Till this day, I long for my wife of sixty years.
I cry a lot. But after the tears, I am still lonely.
Readers, there are millions of us that are lonely today, but we
Are all different. We have our own way of living with loneliness.
Loneliness is like a lost soul in time;
I need not worry about, for I lost my soul when my wife passed,
For my soul went looking for her. Today I have a broken heart
And no soul, but I can always count on loneliness.
Death to me would be a gift today. I can't dance to the music
Anymore, but I can walk with time, for all I have is time and
More time. I realize, loneliness is a large part of life,
A part that we never want to come. But one day, we will look up,
And there it is, looking you in the face.
Now you are all alone.
The sweetest day of your life is with a friend or your spouse.
This is Mother's Day, and I sit alone with no spouse nor friend.
I am the last of all the people I went to school with.
Readers, yes, I am very much alone in this world.
Life will never be fair to some people, no matter how hard you
Try, for every day of your life, you seem to be on trial.

I am sitting on the edge of life, waiting for my time to come.
Every day of my life is yesterday; each day is the same.
Readers, sleep was never a big thing with me, but now I sleep
Very little, perhaps two hours per night.
My wife has been gone, just about three years now, and it seems like
Yesterday. But loneliness is still as strong as day one of
Her death. Can you love a person too much in life? No, you can't.
For there can never be too much love in life. Only if we
Had more love in this world, loneliness would go away.
There are two things in this world that will never set you free:
Loneliness and hate. They kind of go together, for you are always
Alone. I hate being alone. I loved my wife like a mother would
Love her child. I'd done everything in life for her. It was
Called love. Now all I see is her pictures on my wall in the
Living room. At times I would say to myself, Was she ever real?
Is this all in my mind? Was she a stranger in my mind?
This is what loneliness will do to your mind, and I can't let
This take over my mind, for she was so very real. She was the
Love of my life. She was my heart and soul, my life,
Sixty years of sweet life. Yes, we had our ups and downs,
Like most people, but our love was strong and sweet.
To me she was the queen of all women. She could have had any
Man in life, but she went for me. Why? I will never know.
I, till this day, can't thank her enough for
        loving me. And loving me,
She gave me her heart and soul. Now I fight with every day of
Nothing. Readers, there is nothing left for me in life as of
Today, for I can't see past loneliness in this moment of my life.
I don't have the power to say goodbye to my wife.
At times I can smell her presence all around me and feel her
Between the past and present. I just want to hold on to all
Our memories. I understand that there are so many people in
This world who feel just as I feel today. But now I speak for myself,
For I alone must live with loneliness, till I see my wife in
The next life that I hope is near.
My days are long, and my nights are out of this world.

I would treat my wife like the lady she was, every day of her
Life. She was more than just a lady; she was my queen of life.
She was life itself to me. Now loneliness came into play.
It has taken her place in my life. My soul is gone, but my heart
Won't put up with loneliness for too long, for it is weak.
I long for my soul to stop looking for my dear wife and come
Back home to me, and then perhaps we may cope with loneliness
A little longer while I am still here on earth.
My key word today is, rescue me from loneliness, my Lord.
The love we had will always stay on my mind.
She was so lovely; I can't find the words for her. She was out
Of this world. She was my girl, my woman, my lover in life,
My wife most of all, and she belongs to me and only me.
Yes, the love we had for one another will always be in the air.
Readers, I don't wish to cry my heart out
        to you, but I am sure, most
Of you can see how I feel after sixty years of loving one woman.
For there is so much pain, just pain on top of pain, and there
Is loneliness to add to all this pain. How can one cope with this?
The love we had for one another was almost paradise. It was
Our world. We lived in this paradise alone.
For our kind of real love, most people would kill for in life.
So, readers, I ask you, How can I mend my broken heart today?
For I have no soul. It went looking for my departed wife.
For now, it's no longer with me and my heart.
Readers, in so many words, I am a lost soul, living with loneliness.
She meant the world to me. I can't stay here alone anymore.
I need to leave this old world. There is nothing here for me
Anymore. All my hopes and dreams are long gone.
Now it's just loneliness, and I am not in love with loneliness.
It's in love with me and refuses to leave, for there is no future
For us. I reach out for help, but there can be no help after
Your loved one is gone and you are seventy-eight years into the
Future. Is loneliness just a state of mind? Oh no, it's real,
As real as you are today. I wrote the book on loneliness.
Believe me, it's real. It can also kill you or drive you mad.

Yes, readers, it is very real.
I go from day to day, take long rides, and still there is loneliness.
For I eat alone, I walk alone, and I sleep alone. And at
The end, there is loneliness looking at me in the face, saying,
What's next? This is no more than living hell here on earth.
What friends you do have, they don't know what to say to you.
Most likely, it would only upset you even more.
So you see, readers, all you now have is loneliness in life.
I wish I could go back to the way we were,
Just two lovers in life to feed off of one another.
It feels so good to be loved by someone who has given you
Their heart and soul. Oh my god, what a great feeling to be in
Love. There is only four letters in the word *love*,
But you won't find another word on this planet that can take
You from hell to heaven and set your heart free.
Will we ever find another first love? You may find another
Love but never your very first love. That's once in a lifetime.
After you lose a loved one in life, what I am saying to you
Plays a large part in your life today.
Now loneliness will sit in, and you are out there alone.
There're all kinds of loneliness: loss of your pet, your home,
And many other things in life, but the loss of your spouse
After sixty years is another story. There is no bringing back, no one
To reach out to, no one to love or to talk to about your feelings.
And here we are, back at the first step, LONELINESS.
To all the lonely people in this world, we need to come together
And yell out, Give me love, or give me a peace of mind.
Please remove loneliness from our souls.
It's just about a year today for me and am tired of being alone.
I sleep hearing her voice in my ears. The whisper is getting
So much louder, and I get so upset for her love for just one
More time in life, but that will never happen.
Readers, as I sit in my living room, looking at the pictures of
My darling wife, I just want to reach out and hug her or
Someone, anyone. I go back in time when she was just fifteen.
She was my baby girl. Today she still is my baby girl.

Today I just want to reach out to hug someone, anyone,
For I am that lonely. Oh, what a night I have been having.
Please pull loneliness from my heart, just give me peace of mind.
For I long for her love even more today than ever before.
My soul has walked out of my life today looking for the loss
Of my dear wife, for it will never find.
I just want some kind of peace in life for what little time
I may have left. I have taken all her love at the age of fifteen,
And she was so happy. In return she received all of my love.
We were happy in life and became the best of lovers.
We were as one, no more than that, just one person in one body.
Now I hurt so bad. I hurt all over. Even down to my toes, I hurt.
Loneliness is worse than death itself, for you are left alone.
You have nothing left in life, just your pain and loneliness.
I am the keeper of myself, and no one to reach out to.
Somewhere out there, among the stars, she waits for me.
I will wait for my time, for so I hope to be there in her arms.
I have a son who I love very much, but he is not my wife.
He does not drive this vehicle, for he is a passenger in the
Back seat. My wife was the driver of this vehicle to my heart.
She could move me at will. She knew all the gears.
How do you talk to an angel? She was that angel.
When we were young, we would dance the night away under
The stars. Today I just look up at the stars and wonder, Where
Are you, my love? Where are you? May I have one more dance?
Regina, Regina, my darling, I hurt so bad.
The biggest part is now gone to the winds, for I am just a shadow
Of who once was a man.
I just want to feel wanted once more in life, to belong to a
Living soul. I don't want to cry for the rest of my life.
I wanna live life one more time with my dear wife, but that will
Never take place on this earth. But there will be another time
For us, and I will wait for that long day to come. All I have is
Time and loneliness, so I will play the waiting game.
The things we do for love, money can't buy.
My body is like a stopwatch. The ticks came to an end when she

Passed on to the new world, so I will rest the time pice till
We meet in our new world together.
Someday we'll be together, for my star is waiting for me,
And then there will be peace and love in my heart once more.
When I am in the arms of my darling wife,
We all need this resting place after coming off planet earth.
We all need everlasting love into the next world.
Suddenly, as I write, I feel good today. I feel my darling wife.
Regina is looking down at me with her lovely smile, saying, It's
Going to be okay, honey. I could always feel her feeling, and
I can still feel her today. It's called love.
I have taken many long walks, long and winding roads,
Dark roads, at times, I could see no end, the no end to a road
Is just loneliness, playing its part in your life.
Readers, here is the very hard part of your life now is
To keep ahead of loneliness. You must be very strong at all times.
And for myself, I have fallen behind many times. You can't win
With loneliness. It's like the wind; it will always be there.
Even after you are gone, it will find someone else.
All you can do is to stand tall on your own two feet.
If you are lucky to have a good friend, reach out to that person.
That will slow loneliness down for a moment. Life goes on, but
The pain remains. So does your loneliness.
Remember when you were a kid, you would climb a hill and then
Roll down to the bottom. Today I am an adult, and at times my
Thoughts are to climb up a mountain and then start rolling down
That mountainside and hope for an endless drop off to another
World where I could drop off loneliness and leave it behind.
Readers, after my wife's death, I have fallen deeper in love with her.
How can that be even possible? The possibility reaches far past the
Death of one heart and soul, for even after your loss of a loved
One, you can still fall deeper in love with that person. Oh
Yes, you can, my readers. Your heart may stop running, but your
Souls will always be together. That's why my soul is still looking
For its other half, the departure of the woman I love and need.
For today I live and walk hand in hand with loneliness,

And at times I can be very much depressed. I try to keep
Depression off my back most of the time, for loneliness is a
Handful itself. If you have read my other two volumes, then
You also know, Satan is still in my back pocket
Since I was a kid at the age of ten
When I fell into that open grave. Remember that, my readers.
Please don't forget Satan. He plays a large part in loneliness.
Would you want to walk in my shoes today? No, you would not.
My dear, I have a lover's prayer for you.
Here it is, my darling wife:
Please bring me home to you. My door is always open to you.
My darling, my heart cries for the feeling of your soul.
I wish I could reach you by phone, for I would make that
Long different call. Please give me an open line to your ear,
Honey, and then into your heart, for I am like the winds when
It comes to you. My dear, I will move the rivers to walk in the
Path of your love. I would push aside stars to reach for your
Hand. Let my lonely days come to an end, my darling. Just reach
Out your hand to me once more in life.
     Remember, dear, we had it all.
We had each other. So please call on me, honey. Just bring me
Home to you. AMEN, MY DARLING. AMEN.
For now, the SUN is coming up, and it's a beautiful morning, my
Darling. You have given me this lovely day after my prayer.
Thank you, sweetheart. I am forever yours,
And you will forever be my woman wherever you may be. After
Life on earth, we are and always will be together, for we are
Two people in one soul. Let it be written. Let it be done.
And so it will, for my name is KEN, and I demand it.
I know the great power of love, true love,
But I will put it though the test. Can it bring back the love
Of my life to me even after death or take me to her after death?
Some will say, You are out of your mind. Well, most of those people
Know less than I do, so why should I ever listen to them?
Some people can't tell you what day of the week it is,
Or what the principal fact of life is. Do you know, readers?

We can start with the word *love*. You can take it from that
Starting point, for we all need love to jump from day to day.
For what is life without love? We need one another in life.
We need love, that true power of real love.
Pull it together, my readers. It's all about true love in life.
We may not like it, but we need one another, and that is a fact
Of life. And we walk with it every day in life.
Guess what, my people, after all this, there is still loneliness.
Please don't forget loneliness, for it won't forget you.
I say to myself a little prayer every day to be strong.
I have a lot on me. I have loneliness, and I have Satan,
But most of all, I have you, my readers, love and hope that I may
Not be alone. For I adored you, my readers, more than you can
Ever realize.
There will never be another woman in my life like the one
I had, for she was the motor of my soul; she knew all the speeds.
What's going on in this country today? People dying and
Being killed. We now hate one another. We hate everything
Today. We have no real reason for it;
We just move with hate, for hate is everywhere.
But deep, deep down in our hearts, there is just a spark of
Love deep down inside. But today, hate has a foot hole on love.
I can hate everything and everyone, and I don't need a reason.
But to love a person, you need a feeling of that person's heart.
Don't let your mind stand in the way of love.
Listen to your heart. Where there is feeling, there is love.
Hate can't fight with love. Where there is feeling, there is love.
Plus, love will come with help. Feelings will be at the side of
Love. Readers, we need to take back our plants
By putting our love and feelings back out front. Oh, let's not
forget hate, for hate also has help on his side.
LONELINESS works hand in hand with hate.
So you are lonely, depressed, your feelings are gone or
Very low. Now here comes your friend, hate, and hate will say
To you, let's go to the streets and kill someone, anyone.
We are mad at the world. I have loneliness and hate on my side.

For we are now three, loneliness and hate.
For people are scared of us,
We are hate and loneliness together; we can raise hell.
We can hate people. Half the people in this country
Believe in us.
Just take a look out in the streets today.
People are being beaten up and killed.
Let's keep the people in the back seat, for that's where they belong.
Take it from me, for I am Mr. Hate, you
        know me, and Mr. Loneliness.
They say black lives matter. I am Mr. Hate, I can't stop Black
Lives Matter alone. I need all my friends, all you other haters.
I can call on you for help. But there is always love in
Front of me. This is difficult times for the black race.
Thanks to us, loneliness, you and me, Mr. Hate.
Just look around, things seem to be going our way,
They are killing each other every day, and there is no reason
For it. Yes, things are going my way, if I could keep love
Out of our way, because over time, hate will overpower loneliness.
And when it does overpower loneliness, then you just won't care
Anymore, for you will think that you are all alone in this world.
Now you will move toward hate, not by choice but by loneliness.
There is a big difference between being lonely and loneliness.
Take it from me, for I know so well; there is a deep difference.
Readers, remember my first love, the girl I went to school
With, Regina darling. Yes, that was her name. We met at the end
Of a dirt road, where I had to walk to catch the school bus.
Her home was next to the school bus station,
Where we both got on and off. We were both at the young age
Of thirteen. Within two months, we were in love.
There were only a hand full of black kids in this school
Of all white kids. She would take me to swimming parties
At a pond in a field. We had fun, then I would walk her home
Across the fields, a shortcut to her home.
Two miles away, halfway home, there was a sweet strawberry patch
In the center of the field. We both love strawberry.

We would eat berry and kiss and then make love with in strawberry.
Young, sweet love at thirteen, then we would go home.
When she'd get near home, we would break off from one another,
Then she would make a left turn, and I would go to the right,
Down over the hill to the dirt road so her parents wouldn't see
Us together. This went on for one year, at the age of sixteen.
The last day of school for her, I walk up to the end of
The road to see her get on the bus; she was not there.
Her parent found out about us and took her away late the night
Before. Little did I realize, they had other plans for her.
They sold their home and went to Boston.
That was the last I saw my love till forty years later, when
She got off that school bus at this garden center where I was
Working, a bus full of little schoolkids. She was a schoolteacher.
Remember back when she was a young very rich white girl, and we
Had to hide out from her parents, there was no future
Ahead for us because I was a black boy. Then three years later,
When I was sixteen, I put this old car together, and the car
Took me for a test drive out to two states,
Where I met the real love of my life, another REGINA,
A beautiful black Regina at the beach,
I never knew there could ever be another love for me after all.
The days in that strawberry patch,
Where we made love, that was my Regina from the north.
It was so sweet. Yes, over the three years, we were very much
In love. We were going to run away after we finish school,
But her parent had other plans. Back to Regina from the south.
Then my car drove me to my second love, another REGINA.
I, at a very young age, had so much love to give. As a kid,
My heart was so big and full of love. All I knew at that age
Was hard word, as a kid, and hard love.
Then I met my second real love from the south. She was then my
Everything from the first day. It had been three years since I lost
My first love, Regina, from the north.
But the first name was like the second girl I met and fell in

Love with. Her name was also Regina. How
        could this happen to me?
Now, in my heart, there were two Reginas. How can I, a
Sixteen-year-old boy, take all this love, the great love of my first
Love to the white Regina, to another love of a beautiful black
Regina from the south? My love affair with the first Regina
Would be too much for you to understand, my readers,
For it was out of this world. My second, well, that's another
Story. This was over the top. This love went for SIXTY YEARS.
Need I say any more? We were the world's greatest lovers.
Yes, I had the best of both worlds, but Regina from the south
Became the real love of my life for sixty years.
For she was my life, hopes and dreams with her at my side.
I had it all for sixty years. My heart and soul ran over with love.
When I was a kid, we were very poor. I had to drop out of school.
I came up the hard way, and that hard way gave me more education
Than ten years of college. But I got my GED and many
Other things in life.
The big difference between the two women in my life was,
Regina darling, everything was given to her in life as a young
Girl because she was white and rich. She had no worries about
Money or anything in life. It was set aside for her, as
Many times she said to me. My second-love-from-the-south Regina
Came up as I did, very poor. We had to work and fight for
What we needed. We had to think. No one gave us a handout or
A hand down. "She had to use" her brains to provide in life
For herself. Both of my lovers were college girls,
While I was the dropout. But I had two
        Reginas, and one was for sixty
Years as my darling wife in life.
One was a teacher, the other was an English major.
But Regina from the south could outthink the Regina of the
North by a mile. Why? Because she had to work at life. It was
Not given to her. That was the big difference.
But they loved me with all their hearts and souls.
What a lucky man I was in life to have two women that would

Die for me as I would for them. And here I am, still here,
And they are now both gone. Why am I still here?
Well, readers, if you had read my first books, you would understand
That question. Remember me at the age of ten, fallen into
That open grave at midnight, and a cold hand was put on me.
You can take it from there, my readers.
I really don't wish to live anymore. I have lost everything in
Life, the two people that loved me for me. My second Regina
Was the heart of my soul. My soul today is still looking for
Her. And I for Regina of the south, what else can I say?
I really should be going mad at this time in my life.
But I will be around for a while.
After sixty years, Regina was my real lover in life, Regina
From the south. Years do matter.
She was my lady in life and after life.
Readers, remember when my very-first-love Regina from the north,
Came to my workplace many years later on a school trip.
She was a teacher, and once more we met after years,
Forty years. It was for the second time.
It was love all over in a way for both of us, high school love.
She left me with her phone number and address.
Years went by, but I never once called, for she was happy and
Married as I was, and I was madly in love with my wife, Regina
From the south. Regina from the south was my shining star in my
Full love of life. She was all that a woman could be to a man.
And she overstepped by a million miles. She was my real queen,
My true love for sixty years. She was a lady, a woman.
She was my lover in life. She was my better half of life.
She was all the good things God could have given to a person.
Regina from the north was once my other love.
But deep down in my heart, there will always be that love for her,
How can I forget that strawberry patch where we made love at
A very young age? My darling wife from the south, understood
All of this old love I had for Regina from the north.
If I could turn back the hands of time, what would I do differently
From today? Perhaps married them both, Regina from the north

As well as my wife, Regina from the south.
But my heart and soul ran with Regina from the south.
I think perhaps the three of us could have gotten along very
Well in life, but could my heart have taken that much love?
I would have gotten to my knees and cried my heart out
And said, just give it all to me my darling ladies.
Take me, for here I am. For I belong to you both. Just love me
To death. I am still here, my readers, all alone.
Readers, remember the schoolteacher who came to the garden
Center with a bus full of kids. I was standing at the door,
Waiting for it to open with my hand out so no one would fall.
Getting off the bus, my head was down, looking at the steps on
The bus. As she stepped off the bus, I looked up with my hand out,
And she looked into my eyes. At that moment, all we could see
Was that strawberry patch in the field.
Then she fell into my arms, but everyone on the bus thought
She tripped. All that love came back into her heart for me.
In her ear, I whispered to her, "Hi, darling. I still love you."
And she said to me, "Don't ever let me go. Pull yourself
Together, dear, for there are other teachers on the bus,
Plus schoolkids." She had tears in her eyes. All I could see
Was love she still had for me, some forty years later.
She was the Regina from the north. We
        talked about that strawberry
Patch where we made love so many times.
She said to me, "So many times, over the years, I would dream
About our lovemaking in the strawberry patch."
She said, "I still love you so very much." But years have gone
By, and we were both married and very happy.
She said, "I will always love you, my darling." She said, "I must
Love you, for you were my first."
Readers, I keep going back in time for a reason,
For I am all alone today. I lost the two women in my life
Who I loved, Regina from the north and my Regina from the
South. But Regina from the south was my long-running true love.
She rode the roller coaster up and down with many hard roads

Over the sixty years. Yes, she was number one to me in my life.
I love her with all my heart and soul. I feel, if I am drowning
In a sea of love, I just can't help myself today,
For I am the last of the real men. Just ask both of my darling
Loves. But many, many nights and days, I have cried my heart out,
Cried for the Regina from the south. Do you know how I must feel
To lose two loved ones in life and a large part of my
Everyday living? They were not just any two women. They were
Special. They were my lovers of life that were given to me,
Regina from the north, sweet love at thirteen, and my Regina
From the south was the lord queen sent to me.
She was just one of many stars in the sky that was picked
Out and sent down to me. She was my queen
For me, the poor black kid that needed someone like her to walk
With me through life.
At times over the years, the number thirteen keeps coming up,
That strawberry patch. I would say to my wife, "Guess what, dear."
She would say, "That strawberry patch." She knew me that well.
She would say, "Honey, I am in that strawberry
        patch with you now."
I would tell my wife at times about how my old feeling keeps
Coming back into my heart. She would say to me that "okay, honey,
For I know you love me and only me today.
        You may have your dreams,
For I am the one here for you now and will
        be till the end of my time."
Readers, this story is all about MEMORY and LONELINESS.
I will get to that later in my story. So let me tell you
A little more about me and my wife, Regina from the south.
Readers, I am very lonely is the real name for all of us.
That means you also, my readers. It can drive you mad.
After a while, you will hate everything. You will then start
To feel sorry for yourself. You will then see the world in front
Of you with no one in it but you and loneliness.
Every day is empty for you in life. It can all be a living hell.
Just think about it, you lost two loves of your life.

One was a real angel, Regina from the south.
So tell me, my readers, just how should I feel—dead inside,
Nothing to live for, nothing. So I reach out to heaven for
The love I have lost. Just reach down with your hand, and tell
Me it will be soon for me, for I will be with the woman I so love.
I just want to feel her love tonight in my heart.
Regina from the south, I need you, my darling. Just give me
A drop of your love till we meet once more at your place in
Heaven. I know you still feel my love for you, darling.
You must still feel all my love for you, for we were as one
In life. My soul left me a while back when looking for you.
It must be near to you by now. When it reaches for your hand, I
I will also feel your love once more, my darling Regina.
For our love will never end. We ride with time, my darling,
And there is no end to time. Hold on, dear. I am near.
I will reach for your hand soon, darling.
Someone, please take me from this old world into the new life
With my wife, Regina from the south. I long for every drop of
Her love. Just let me kiss the feet that she walks on in heaven.
At times I feel so close to death, and for me, that's a good thing.
For I am sick of loneliness. I can't even sleep alone,
For there is loneliness. At one time in my life, I had paradise,
For I had my darling wife, Regina from the south, in my life.
Today I have nothing but loneliness.
I know I may not be all alone, for some of my readers may also
Feel loneliness. If so, then you understand how I feel today.
I just sit in my living room, seven days and nights, looking at
The eight pictures on my walls of my darling wife, Regina from
The south. I just sit and talk to her. I cry most of the time.
She can be so real to me on that wall.
At times I get up, walk over, and kiss each picture on that wall.
I would say I am losing my mind. Or am I a slave of loneliness?
Some may say I am going out of my head. No, I am still much
Too strong to lose it as of yet. But this loneliness is a
Sick dark world of its own. It can take you from end to end in
A moment. Take it from me, for I once lived with it for two years.

As I said to you a long time back in my first book, I am not a
Writer, but I can tell you the story of my wife and myself.
I don't need to be a writer to tell the TRUTH of a real story.
The PEN in my hand is the writing tool in my hand of the truth.
All I need to do is pick up the pen in my hand and then tell
The story. Is it me telling the story, or is it my wife?
I hope it's my wife, for she is better than I. She is the queen of love.
Her love moves the pen in my hand. I can't do this alone.
When she was unable to walk up the steps alone, I would stand
Behind her for support. At times she would fall back on me
And then give me a big kiss and laugh.
She knew for sure that I had her back, just like I had her back
In real life. We were like one person in life, just one body.
She would say, "If you should leave me in life, I would be the same."
"Dear, in this life, I will never leave you or in the next life.
Don't you ever think that, for I am your lover till the end."
She would then smile and say, "Yes, darling." But now all that is
Gone, just me and loneliness and you, my dear readers,
And, yes, good old Satan. Please don't forget him.
He is behind everything that went wrong in our lives.
I am at the top of his list. I don't wish to talk about him today.
Today I must deal with loneliness. Nothing feels right anymore.
To me, I have no feeling for anyone or anything,
That's what loneliness can do to a mind. I no longer have love
In my life to turn me around, just loneliness, trying to run me
Over the edge. Perhaps the pictures on the walls of my
Wife stand in front of loneliness, for that is all I have.
I have my wife's ashes in two boxes under her pictures that
I kiss every day. I still have some of her with me in life.
I'll always love my wife. Some may say I need help. I need to
Get out and find other people. My answer to that is NO, NO, NO.
Will I find another Regina from the south? The answer is no.
I will sit this trip out alone, not really alone, for I have
Loneliness. Readers, this is all about loneliness and what it
Can do to a person. Thank God, I have you, my readers.
Sometimes I say to myself, Where did our love go?

I don't even know what day of the week it is anymore.
Why should I? For there is no love in any day of the week for me.
For every day is the same, just loneliness and I.
Loneliness is all I have. It will stand by me day and night
I can depend on that. A few supernatural things have taken
Place with me in my life, starting at the age of ten.
You should know the rest, my readers, if you have followed me in
My sixty years, for it have taken everything that I loved from
Me in life. Now it's just me to stand toe to toe with loneliness
And its friend, Satan.
I think I will write a letter to my wife and put a stamp on it
And say address unknown. Let it go to the winds
And see if heaven will pick it up and drop it off in Regina's mail
Box to the lovely Regina from the south of Maryland.
For some day we will be together. I feel this in my heart.
And so does my wife, for she is a special part of me.
For she was my life, my full life.
If I can't have her back, then I just want to be friends with
Her spirit. I will never have another woman in my life,
For she took all my love with her, and I am glad of that.
I feel she will never be alone as long as my love is with her.
Now I have no soul, for it's on a hunt for my wife,
So you see is my readers without a soul, there is no love for another.
The light is out in my heart. The thrill is gone now.
All I have now is loneliness. It was once a wonderful life for
Me in the way of love, for I had Regina from the south, my wife.
At times she would kiss me and take my breath away.
She said to me one time, "I could stop your heart if I look hard
Into your eyes, for I have that much love for you in my heart."
In my heart, it rains every day, and a dark cloud covers my mind,
Like dust falling from the sky. I have a hard habit to break,
Loving an angel, a habit I wish to live with till we meet
For the second time. She is so unforgettable.
She was like a river of love, running through my heart,
Then you would fall to your knees and cry
        out, "I love you, darling."

I love you, readers. I have taken three weeks out from
Telling my story. Loneliness came down very hard on me
Because I feel better when writing and telling my story.
This does not replace loneliness, and I became depressed.
And today is Monday, just one day out of seven.
But every day is Monday to me; they are all the same.
Loneliness rides with each day of the week. I now
Have been married to loneliness for a full two years
Now, and I see no getting away. There are so many people
Out in the world just like me. Loneliness will live
In many homes and will lean on millions of people
Who are alone and lonely. And then loneliness will
Come into your life as it has done so many times.
My readers, I will tell you later in my story how
You can bring loneliness to a stop. There is a way.
After you have lost a loved one, like I have for sixty
Years, or any time in your life, you are now at a point
Where you don't care anymore. Now depression sets in.
And then here come Mr. Loneliness. The big part of my
Story is about loneliness, for I have lived it.
Who can better tell you the story of loneliness than I,
And the way it makes you feel every day and every night
Of your life? I know I am not alone in this world with
Loneliness. But no one person is the same. We all
Don't have the power to climb a mountaintop or roll
Out from loneliness. There is a difference of feeling
And thinking between people, but we are all still
Part of the human race.
I had to see my doctor last Tuesday. I felt a little
Under the weather. My doctor said, "You need a friend."
I HAD TO LAUGH. I CAME IN TO SEE HER BECAUSE I WAS
Under the weather, not for a friend. My doctor is only
Twenty-two years old. I have a toothbrush older than
The doctor. I said, "Doc, I have no friends. They are all
Gone." She said, "What do you mean?" "Doctor, they are all
Dead. I am the only one left." Then she said to me, "Find

Another friend in life." As I listened to my doctor, I was
Saying to myself, "After today, I will have a new doctor."
Readers, just a little line about my doctor, even doctors
Can be wrong at times. You must listen to yourself.
Only you know your body and mind.
So I went looking for another doctor, someone with a little
More age on life. Readers, do you know how long it takes
In life to have a real friend? A lifetime.
If you are lucky, real friends are hard to come by.
I could have a cup of coffee with you, and then could
I call you a friend? The answer would be NO.
That's a five-dollar friend for the coffee.
A real friend would have your back for life. Why am
I telling you all of this? Because it's real.
A real friend will walk that last mile with you, even
In the rain. That's a real friend, my readers.
For me to find a real friend today would take a lifetime.
That I don't have. I only live from moment to moment,
Not day to day, just moment to moment. At eighty years,
My glass is just about out.
This old heart of mine is just about out of time.
And the light inside of my heart is very dim;
Most of my sunny days are long gone now. I just live for the
Moment. Any moment in life now is good for me. Being alone in
The world is a living hell. Everyone needs someone in life.
I had that, loving someone for sixty years.
I can never get that back in life, for she is now gone from my
Life, the life we once had. We had deep love down to our souls.
Most people can't say that today. We were the classic lovers of
All times, and my doctor told me to get a friend.
What a joke that was. I am the very last of the real lovers.
I know what it takes to love a real woman, not just the play in
Bed, not sex alone, the smile, the kiss, to hold her hand in
The time of need, just to look her in the eyes and say, "Darling,
I love you. I would walk to hell and back for you, my darling."
That special person comes only once in a lifetime.

You may have love in your life but never that one special
Person. You will know if she or he is that special one in your
Life. Yes, time together will tell. Say to yourself,
Would that person walk ten miles in the rain for me if you were
Sick? In your heart, will be that answer.
I have many good dreams in my life to remember.
All I can do today is sit and dream, dream of all the good
Times I had with my wife. No one can take that from me, not
Even loneliness.
Sometimes when we touch, our love would run a river called hot
Love. One can't find that today.
Walking with my wife was like walking in rhythm.
My heart would sing, and my soul would dance alongside me.
It was like a natural high. Yes, I love that lady more than life
Itself, that lady, Regina from the south of Maryland.
I died a thousand times after her death.
Maybe tomorrow will be my day to die. I can only hope so,
For the one I loved is gone. There's no need for me to be here
Anymore. The angel of mine went home. I now wait for my ride.
For I am lost in her love. On rainy days, we would make love.
Sometimes it was all in our minds, and we could work with that.
Sometimes you just can't help falling in love with that special
Person that walked into your life. At that moment, it will be
always and forever. Sometimes I would get misty as I looked
Into her eyes or kissed her lips.
Readers, loneliness you don't see, but loneliness is a feeling
That will run deep down into your heart and soul.
It can break you or kill you, but here is where real love comes
Into play. The key word is love. Take me after sixty years
Of true love, real love. Loneliness will only slow you down,
May even keep me to myself but will never take the love of my
Dear wife out of my mind and heart. She will always be with me.
To me loneliness is just a part-time rider,
Not a lover. Remember that, my readers, love is a very beautiful
Thing, real love that is. It's the greatest thing in life.
At times real love can be greater than life.

Without love in your life, then what is life to you? Just another day,
Another year. Without real love, every day and year means nothing.
Gee whiz, people, love and life must go together. I can still smell
My wife's sweet scents all in the air.
Her body odor will never leave me. I know her, and we will get
Together in the next life, and we will pick up where we
Left off. I long for her love. I long for her sweet smells
And the look she had in her eyes. I am no longer lonely when I am
Writing, for she brings love to my heart.
It's when I put down the pen, loneliness finds its way back into my
Life. We were so in love. We could walk on water for
One another. We felt our love was that strong.
All of our feelings ran into each other's body, like water running
Down a hill, then we just fell in love again and again.
Understand me now, readers, love is the ruler of life, NOT hate.
We bring on that hate for no reason at all,
But love is and will always be close to your heart and soul.
Hate will never be in the heart, only in the mind.
People can talk your mind into wild things,
But they can never talk your heart into anything.
Your heart will always be loved and will remember love even after
Death.
Remember when loneliness came into your life.
It will only be in your mind, not your heart. It can never
Overrule love that will always be in your heart.
Readers, OH, what a night I had last night. After I put down the
Pen when I finished writing, loneliness came on to me very strong.
My head felt like it was ready to blow up, all because I
Was free of it writing my story. When I am writing, there is no
Room for loneliness. Only when I stop, here it comes. My only
Execute is to write and to keep writing to hold off loneliness as
Long as my pen will hold out, and I have many pens in my house.
Do you understand the saying, my readers?
Listen to me, my readers, for I have found the key to loneliness.
It will only last for a while, but it will give you that peace of
Mind for a moment. Write about someone or somebody you love.

When you are writing, there is no room in your mind for loneliness.
Write about a friend, a pet dog that you once had,
Anything to fill your mind. If your mine is full, there is no
Room for loneliness. Now this won't last forever. Hobbies,
Anything to fill your mind, the key is, don't open your mind to
Loneliness. It took me two years of hard times to find the key
To loneliness, for I had no help, as I am giving it to you.
Memories are also very good for the mind. Memories are the best.
Not only will it keep out loneliness, it's also very good for the
Heart. If you are alone, like I am today, think about your precious
Love that you once had in life, for I had sixty years of precious
Love. Remember, readers, what I have said to you over the years
Many, many times as we go back in my
          books. You must read volume
One and volume two before you can understand volume three.
Remember what I said to you not to forget:
LOVE IS THE KEY TO LIFE. Love overrules everything on this
Planet earth, not hate, LOVE. For love is god all power on
This earth. We have the power to overcome just about anything.
As long as we have love in our hearts, love is the great power
Deep down in our hearts. There is no place in the heart and soul
For HATE. Your GOD had seen to that. Hate
          can only work on the mind
If you let it. Readers, I believe the best of my life and love
Is yet to come in the next world with my darling wife.
Earth is only a step off for all of us.
IT is a tool for us to get ready for the next life,
The everlasting life among the stars, where we will dance
And make everlasting love throughout the galaxy of all the
Great people who went in front of us.
But we will be two of the great lovers of all times,
For we will walk and talk, dance among the
          stars, and look down and
Smile. And so will you, my readers. And we will say we are
Horne now, my dear. We will run with endless time.
I now have endless years to say how much I love you, my darling,

Time that will reach across the galaxy of love,
Love that will never stand still, for we will dance on and on
With endless time. What a good thing that will be, my darling.
Readers, this is still about loneliness. We are still on this earth.
Remember, back in our history books, give me life or give me death.
Without love, you walk with loneliness,
And that is next to death.
At times your emotion can run very high. You need to just
Stop and take a MINUTE.
All I can say to you on the tip of my tongue is to keep a full
Mind from loneliness. You can even write to me
Now that one for the road. But, yes, you can write me if need be,
For you were with my wife and I for sixty years.
I could be the ideal person, who better than I,
For I have been to the gates of HELL twice, had Satan sit on
My chest. I took a fall into an open grave at midnight
When I was just a kid at the age of TEN. Then when I had the
Hand of Satan on my back, after that, nothing in life was the same
For me. So who better could you talk to on this planet?
Readers, I think we need one another.
People, we need to keep our heads looking up, not down,
For we are our own keeper, no one else, just us.
We can give loneliness a run for its money.
        Every day we can overcome.
Love is always on your side if you have a heart, and we DO.
Then love will always be there. That comes with life.
Love is the big picture on this earth,
I am with you, my readers. We will stand tall with the power
OF love in our hearts. We may be alone now, but we are never
Losers in life. We have a heart and a soul,
OR I had a soul at one time, till it went looking for my wife.
But that's okay with me.
Readers, we are not helpless; we are just lonely.
And at times our emotion will try and run wild.
Sometimes I say to myself, "Who's holding my wife now in heaven?"
No one, I hope, for she belongs to me on earth and in heaven.

This I'm sure she knows. She took all my love with her to the
Next life. I would want it that way. With all my love in her
Heart, she would never be alone, for she will never pass this way
In life again here on earth.
But she will wait for me as she had done once before in life.
In heaven, she is a queen, my queen. My soul may reach her before
I do, and that will be just fine. She would be very happy,
And it would remain with her till I come home.
My wife was the only person on this earth that could make me
Laugh. She said to me one day, "I can also make you cry."
"Just how would you do that, my lady?"
She looked into my eyes and said, "I don't love you anymore."
I then fell to my knees, crying, "Please don't leave me."
She said, "Am only joking, dear. I would never leave you in life."
But the joke was on me, for I was crying for real. She said, "Am
So sorry, honey. I should have never said that." That's okay, dear,
For I know you are in my heart forever as I am yours.
Yes, my darling, we are as one and only one here on this earth.
Readers, I just don't want to be lonely anymore. I just want to
Be loved by the woman I once had in life.
She was the best wife any man could wish for in any lifetime,
Sixty years of true love, all from the heart.
But in my life now, at my age or any age, there will never be
Another woman like my lovely wife, Regina.
Funny how time slips away. I am gonna kiss her for every day that
I have left in my life. Nobody knows the dead feeling I have
In my heart today, for my soul is no longer with me. It's looking
For Regina, and that I understand. At one time my heart was full
Of rich love for the woman in my life. Now there is nothing but
Loneliness. And, yes, my readers, we know all about loneliness.
I say amen to all the lonely souls who may have lost a loved
One in life. As I said, we must keep a full mind to keep out
Loneliness. That's not an easy job, but it's a must to all of us.
Readers, even after sixty years, I still have so much I wanted
To tell my wife. There is never enough time in life for love,
Sixty years more to say how much more we all love our wives.

There is no end to true love. Love is like time.
Love will follow your heart and soul and will pass you in life.
As a human, we are on a time clock, running with love. As we run
Out, love is still there and will always be there.
For there is no time clock for love.
Love will run with time throughout the next life.
The threat will always be with us for losing a loved one.
I can't explain it. Yes, I can see ahead.
Most of it is not good. The world is in a bad place today,
For what little time I have left on this earth, I can't
See the world getting any better. Hate now is in the driver's
Seat. What the world needs now is love, deep deep love to stop
Hate. But it can be done, my readers. We have this in our hearts.
But hate is in our minds. We can, and we must derail hate
With all the love in our hearts. We were put here on this earth
To love one another. We were to love, not to hate one another.
This is the work of mankind. Hate spreads like wildfire,
And now it is out of control. There is a thin line between
Love and hate. At times, things can be very easy for two and
So hard for one. After you lose your loved one in life,
Readers, as I said in my other two books, the great storm is
Coming, like we have never seen before in life.
It will be the storm of all storms. The last one we will ever
See. But there's still time for us, people.
We need to bring back love, lots of love.
Readers, love is not something you find; LOVE FINDS YOU.
My wife was high test. Her love was real, and she only ran off
High-test love. Now I just sit on the sidelines, for there is no
High test to run my body.
My heart looks for that high test to run through my heart and
Soul in order for me to start up the love I once had.
No, I am not out of gas, but my love is gone. My body was once
Like a high-performance car that ran in top speed when it was
Full of high-test love, for now I can't run off of unleaded love.
It's called artificial love, false love. I can't climb a mountain
Of love on false hopes. I will never, at my age, find another

True love in life, for my days are numbered.
I realize this more than anyone, for I lost all hope.
That love I once had will never return, so I just sit on the
Sideline, out of high-test love. The motor in my heart
Is on its last beat or last leg. Each day I slow down just a
Little more. I can't climb another hill in life.
This old body has seen its better days. At one time, I could
Run with the best of them. Now it's hard
        for me to get out of the way.
Today I had a hard time just to make it to the bathroom.
There will never be another real thing in my life.
True love is only once in a lifetime. I almost had it in the
Strawberry patch. Today I am glad it was not the strawberry
Patch for me. Regina from the south was the real lady in my life.
But little did I realize, my true love was waiting for me,
Regina from the south. Was it magic? No, it was true love that
Found me on the beach in Maryland on a lovely hot day.
Today I drift along with loneliness, once in a while,
Aimlessly in time. One could say I am just a drifter in time,
For I have seen more than most, perhaps more than anyone on
This earth. At times I wonder, is there a reason for me to be
Still here on this earth? I don't care to be here.
What else do you want from me? I ask myself.
Today, once more, I reach out my hand to you, my Lord. Please
Bring me home to my wife, but I know we don't always get what we
Want, for I loved her yesterday, I love her today, and I
Will love her throughout time. That's real love.
Today my smile is just a frown, upside down,
For me to have faith. How can I, for you took all my love from
Me, all my hopes and dreams. Can you understand how I feel
Today? But I have my loyal readers,
Who have been with me for more than sixty now.
If I can't be with my wife, then give me the power to be
A distant lover. Just let me have a spark of her love.
That would put some life back into this old heart,
Just a taste of high test once more in this old broken-down heart,

Let me get to the next base in my life, Lord.
Let me catch up with my long-lost soul, and we will
Walk together to our home plate, for I loved that woman for so
Many reasons. And in my heart, she was all seasons.
Readers, as you know in my past life, I was a king,
A proud black king, but there was no Regina back in that life.
If Regina was in my past life, I could have ruled the world with
Her beauty.
When I was very young, I went to work with holes
In my shoes. Take off one shoe, you could look down at the ground.
I guess you could call me a black beast. Sometimes I had no
Lunch. I would eat out of a trash can, but I never told my wife,
For she was the beauty of my life, beauty and the beath.
Many days, as a black man, I was running scared,
But there was no time to stop for a black man.
We were then very young lovers, and I just wanted her to be
Happy. I would do anything to keep her safe and happy.
If that means eating out of a trash can at times, then so be it.
I would work from sunup to sundown.
There were no steady jobs for a black man in the day.
You took only what you could get. No day was the same for a
Black man. Would we eat tomorrow? MAYBE.
Would I have a job the next day? MAYBE. Most black jobs for
A black man were labor jobs,
Jobs white men wouldn't take. He was much
        too good for a labor job.
He had the black man for that job, fifty cents per hour,
And you done the work of two men in one day, at the end of a
I would go and lie down someplace before I went home
Just to rest. When I got home, my wife would say to me,
"How was your day, dear?" MY answer was,
        "It was a good day, dear."
But she knew better than that. She knew me, but she kept it
All inside. Then later in life, I started working for myself.
Things were a little better. You know the rest, my readers.
It's all about loneliness today.

When I was a very young boy, I would walk
        in the woods and sit next
To a large tree and dream about a beautiful young girl in my
Life. Yes, I would dream many, many times for this young girl.
What would she be like? Would a girl like that want me?
I would look up at the top of a tall tree and say to this tree,
"Can I, this poor little boy, find a sweet little girl that would
Perhaps love me later in life?"
Then I would say to myself, "There can be no girl like that
Would want me." Just the very thought of this
Was a wild dream. Today I was fifteen. I didn't even own a pair
Of shoes. No, this girl of my dreams would never look at me.
I was poor and just a black kid, but I had a very big heart,
A very big heart, and I would look for this girl of my dreams.
Remember now, the girl of the north was taken away from me
At night, at the end of her school year.
A year later, I found the true love of my life at the beach
In Maryland. This was the real girl I was dreaming of in
The woods when I was sitting next to this large tree, and I
Was looking up and talking to this tree.
I wanted this girl so much that at times, next to this tree,
I could feel the earth move under me, and I would yell
Out and say, "Hey, lovely girl, for I am coming for you.
Wherever you may be, I'll find you, and you will be my wife."
And so it happened. I found my girl, my true Regina in life.
And then love was everywhere. Love was in the air,
It was all round us, for we were young lovers till this day.
We are still lovers, but today old lovers.
Love will run with time, my readers. Only humans get old and die.
But love never dies. It will run till the end of time.
Each day in life is another moment in time for love to another
Person, just like we can't stop time, nor can we stop love.
What a beautiful world this could be if we all were in love,
For love overrules hate. With all our love, as people, we could
Run hate right off this planet.
All we need to do is pull our love together. Just say "hi, friend,"

To one another. Just give that lovely smile when you walk by,
And watch hate take a back seat. We just don't want him in
The back seat. We want hate off this planet.
There is no place for hate anywhere on this planet.
Even the loss of a good friend or a spouse after many years,
With love in the air all around you, then loneliness will slowly
Go away after a little while. We will never forget our loved ones,
But with love in the air, we would feel a little better.
Like I once said, give me love or give me death.
(Was it I who wrote those words?)
Readers, I say all this to you, for if you had the kind of love
In your life, as I once had, then loneliness will have a very
Hard time sitting beside you in life.
At times I will take a walk in the night and look up at
The stars. If one would blink, then that's my darling wife
Winking at me. It would then bring tears to my eyes,
And I would say to that star, "We're gonna make it, dear.
We'll be together soon. For today I walk against all odds."
My wife was the only one who really knew me.
There is nothing worse than being alone. I don't cry out
Loud; I just keep it inside me
And hide my feeling. These eyes have seen a lot of love,
But no more will they see another like I had with her.
It's like lookin' through a window, but there is nothing there.
I want to know what love is once more in life.
I want to feel her love once more in my lifetime.
I want this love from my darling Regina from the south.
All the love has gone, only memory of that love today.
But my love is still in flight on its way to Regina, my darling,
For it may catch up with my soul, for its still looking for
My soulmate, Regina. As I grow older, my love grows even
Stronger for the woman I lost. Sometimes I write her a letter
And drop off in the mailbox,
Address unknow to Regina Murrey, my darling wife.
Dear, if you should get this letter, I am still waiting for my ride.
Please send me the next train, for there is a fork in the road.

Perhaps I was waiting on the wrong side of the road,
So I will step to the other side for my ride.
Dear, the nights are long and dark. The days are bright and
Lonely. Please rush my ride to me, for I long for your love
Once more in my heart. Dear, can you ack a little more
Swiftly with my ride?
When you have real love, every day is something new. Every day
Is precious love. You then say to yourself, "Heaven must have
Sent her to me." When I walk, I keep looking back, but my
Darling wife is not in sight. Readers, I sleep very little anymore,
About two hours per night. It's just a waste of time for me in
This life. At times I feel like a lonely wolf in the woods.
Readers, there is a thin line between love and real love, and
There is a thin line between love and hate.
It all comes from the heart, not the mind. Readers, our day will
Also come. We all have a day set aside for each one of us,
But never when we are ready. But are we ever ready?
For I only speak for myself. Yes, I am more than ready.
Readers, hope begins when you stand in the dark, looking
Out at the light, for I still have hope.
Now I wait for the love train, for that train will show me
The light from the dark side of my heart.
Readers, how do we survive in this world today? My readers,
It's very hard to overcome at times. We need love.
We also need one another. We need to get behind this train
And push love for the good of all people.
We need to make up many years of lost love. We have given
Mr. Hate a free hand. We have given hate the freedom of speech,
The voice to yell out and to overcome. Mr. Hate today is all
Over TV, in the streets, even in our homes. There is no real
Peace on this planet today. There are wars all over the world.
We are fighting over land that was here long before mankind
And will be here long after we are gone, but yet we still
Fight over what we will never own in life.
We are pushed by hate, greed, and loneliness. They are
In the driver's seat today, and we let this happen to a point

We take our foot off the pedal, so we are now freewheeling
In life, while Mr. Hate is in overdrive.
We need to get back on the pedal of love and put the gear
In superdrive. We must run down Mr. Hate.
Now, people, today this must be done. We are running out of time.
We need love back in our lives.
Life can be messy at times. It shows us who we really are
And who we can be in life. Life itself is not a guideline
To success in life. The achievement of something desired
By attempt of love is from your heart.
Our heart will always be the drineing forth in life.
So much have changed in life from the way it used to be,
But love will always be in your heart, for we are not alone
In this world. Kook around you; there are other people just
Like you. We need each other. Come, my readers,
Let's march on Mr. Hate together.
We can run him out of town. Just to be in love is nothing
More than true love. Love is all-power here on earth.
Love is the real answer to living on this old earth.
Just to be close to your loved ones in life is peace in
Your hearts and minds. Just to have good friends can be love,
To make a phone call when you are lonely and say, "Hi, friend,"
That's love from your heart. Just to feel good will put a smile
On your face and in your heart for a moment.
It's a joy in life to have real love and that all we really need
In our hearts for the moment of love at any given time will
Make you smile. Then everything is coming up love,
But loneliness will still play a very large part in your life.
Now that you are alone, you then become weak. You feel there is
No hope. All your dreams are gone. Now you are open for anything
In life. I know this, my readers, for I was once there.
Now here comes what you really don't need in your life, loneliness.
But for now, you are open for anything. Again, my readers, I was
Once there, so I am telling you the story so you may understand.
There is a way out. Please don't get me wrong, I still have hard
Times, but I know now how to deal with it.

There is one thing for sure, my readers; we won't pass this way
Again in life. If you were anything like me in life, once you
Lost your spouse, then you were wide open for loneliness.
I was, so am telling you what may take place in your life after
The love of a loved one. That's what this story is all about,
My true story. There's no time limit allowed on a broken heart.
So let me go on with my story. Sometimes I get offtrack just to
Speak to my reader as a personal human being.
Do you realize how long Mr. Loneliness has been around?
Before time. Yes, it was here before time.
Does that answer any question that one may
        have about Mr. Loneliness?
He has removed many lonely souls from this earth.
He is no friend to us, my readers. Mr. Loneliness leans on the
Very weak, but we have each other, my readers,
Writing my story does help to ease my pain, but at times
I do get offtrack, for it feels so good to talk to someone,
Even if it is in my story. This story is all about memories.
Loneliness is no friend to us, my readers. I said this to you
Once before, and I will keep saying.
You have me, my readers, if you should need a friend.
Now you are saying to yourself, the nights are better, for
I have found loneliness. No, my friends, you did not find loneliness;
Loneliness found you. He was waiting for someone like you.
Take it from me, for I was that very lonely person, and I still
Am at times. History tells us that life is a chronological
Record of events, but love will always find a way.
You know, readers, when you get right down to it, love will
Always find a way. I can go back and see reflections of so
Many good years we had that will always be good memories.
Memories are all over my heart,
For I still have my ups and downs. It's gonna take a miracle to
Ever overcome the loss of a loved one, maybe never,
But I am now in control of my mind. It took a while for me
To understand how loneliness can work on a broken heart.
It goes straight to the mind, then later to the heart.

But as I said, there is a way out. Memories that we all have
Keep your mind busy. A busy mind have no place for loneliness.
Readers, emotions can be a good thing in life. Think about the
Good times you once had. Think of all the good memories.
Nothing is so difficult in life when you have good memories.
Think of all the good, loving times with your spouse
Or your friends. That's what I do each and every day.
Nothing can take that from your heart, not even loneliness.
I used to say to my darling wife, just be my lady in life.
She would look at me and say, "I am much more than your lady.
I am your everlasting lover in life.
I will be at your side throughout all times, darling,"
And, yes, she was at my side of every day of her life,
And somewhere out there, she is still at my side and in my heart.
She is my shining star.
I look up in the skies at her as still my superstar.
She was a classic soul here on earth,
For, readers, we can never walk away from love,
And we will meet in the next world. Life is very good when you
Are in love. We can't live without it.
But life won't last forever, and no one said to you life will
Be fair. Life can be very hard at times.
It will take all your friends from you in life, and it will
Sometimes take your loving spouse, who you loved over many years.
Now it's back to you, just you alone. Just keep your memory out
Front. Think of all the good years you once had together.
No one can take that from you. Good memory
        will always be with you,
For you and only you own those memories.
I can still hear her softly with her songs in my ears.
Readers, if you don't know me by now, then you will never
Understand me by now. And I hope you do
understand me, for I am real.
Readers, I can call myself the POSTMAN; I only send letters to
My wife as unknows, but you can read all the pages in my books,
Talking about life, my life, and the life of my dear wife.

Yes, we know all about life and then some,
For most people are the same wherever you go in life.
They just want to be loved and to have real love.
Things do happen to you in life, which is no fault of your own.
It's called unfair life. Readers, you know what happened to me
At the age of ten, where I fell into that open grave,
And nothing has been the same for me in life, the only good thing
Was the love of my wife that was taken from me.
I still have Satan in my back pocket, and there is nothing
I can do about it. I have been to the gates of hell twice
In my lifetime. The only thing that kept me out of the gates
Of hell was the love of my wife, for she had the Lord on her side.
But I don't. So where do I go from here, my readers?
I pray the gates of hell will never happen to you by reading
My books. Satan is not my best friend.
Readers, I do like the sound of the postman, for I do write my
Wife every now and then, for I must write her.
Since my wife's passing, I have walked a many dark roads in my
Mind, but they have all come up the same in my mind.
There is no end to the night of darkness.
There will come a day, darkness will be overruled by the
Light of love in my heart.
Readers, they say, men don't cry. I am the last of the real men,
But I have cried a million times since my wife's death.
I will tell that to the world. My wife is worth a million tears.
If you were in love, then you are sure to cry if it was real
Love. True love will bring out the tears.
How can you not cry if there are feelings there?
To feel a little better, you must cry a tear. You must bring
Out that love, for it will only build up in your heart and
Break you down. Just let it all out, and you will feel a little
Better. I still cry at nights to myself. When the wind blows,
I get very upset, for I think it could be my dear wife saying,
"Hello, darling," for she will always be in my heart. The love we
Had will never go away. It was too real. That kind of love will
Travel with you even after death. It's not for me to say true love

Won't travel, for in my heart, it will travel on after life.
Look at my soul, for it took off after the death of my dear
Wife, Regina, and we were made for each other. Our hearts and
Soul were as one. As you can see, my soul is on the march.
Readers, you know the old saying,
There's a thin line between love and hate. We must get love back.
We must unite together with all our love. We need one another
Today, my readers, more than ever. Readers, I have love on my mind
From sunrise to sunset. I keep her love on my mind and in
My heart day and night. I just can't help myself, nor would
You if you had the love we had. With that kind of love, there is
Very little room for loneliness.
All of my young age, I was waiting for a girl like her,
Regina from the south. She was one in a million. She was that
Woman in my life, for she was the queen of all women on this
Earth. For I believe she was born for me and only me.
I believe that with all my heart, for she took my heart and
Soul. And my soul is still on the lookout for my Regina.
She was a legend in her time and will be in the next world.
Once more, I say, I am the last of the real men. WHY?
For I have been to hell in my young days. I have been to
The gates of hell. I had Satan sit on my chest.
I had his hand on my back when I fell in that open grave.
I own the right of the last real man on earth,
For I am now on my own in life.
Readers, back to loneliness, we now know all about loneliness,
Don't we? We understand how it works, how it will slowly take
Over your mind, and we now know how to keep our mind full.
Yes, it's a very hard job. I never said it was easy, but we can
Get past it because we have our memories, many good memories.
When you can't find anything to do, just call on those good
Memories;
They will always be in your heart. They will forever be in
You as well, for your heart will go on in life. You can't
Stop love; all you need to do is say, "Move out, loneliness. Here

Comes my memories." You can do that
        anytime you wish, my readers.
Just open your heart and mind and fall back on your memories,
It's late at night, and you are lonely, and now you feel loneliness
Moving in. Just call on your memories to hold on till morning
Comes. At daylight, things seem a little clear. Darkness is
Very to deal with, I know.
Readers, I am so proud of my past life with my wife, Regina from
The south. She was my queen in today's world.
Readers, time is tight in my heart, for my love is gone.
But still I have memory, but they are not like the real thing.
Today, readers, love is gone from most of this world. Just
Look around you; everything is bad news, plus good news don't sell.
So love is gone from most of us. Thanks to the news today.
And the gates are now open for Mr. Hate and his friends
So that now comes into your mind and heart. But, my friends,
Even with all that, love is still the great fight on this earth,
Love always will be the great power of all times.
Look at me; I passed death eight times in life. No thanks to
Satan. Thanks to the love of my wife; I am still here.
I should be in the den of hell, but my wife said no to Satan.
So today I float on in life.
I also had many experiences with Mr. Hate over the last two years.
To explain, Mr. Hate is only one word, LOVE and more of our LOVE.
Today most love is gone from the world picture. What's wrong
With us today, people? Is there no love left in our hearts today?
I would hate to think that of us as the people of this world.
Listen, people, never give up, NEVER. That's not in the cards for us,
For you have love on your side. It will never leave your heart.
Love is the number one fighter in your heart.
Readers, I talk to you as my friend, for I have never met any
Of you, but you have been my readers for over sixty years now.
I wish to bring that smile to your face as I write my story,
For life is not all bad, for there is love, and we need one another.
My readers, remember, all women are special. They are all special
Ladies in this life. And if you are lucky, you just may fall in

Love with that special lady in your life.
For I fell and am still falling although she is no longer with me.
But I love her even more. She may be gone, but her love will
Live on throughout time.
Once more I say to you, my readers, give me everlasting love,
Love or give me DEATH. As I said, love never stops.
It was here before time, and it was around before mankind.
Today is a special day for me because the wind is in my ears.
My wife is saying, "I love you, my darling. I will blow by
Every now and then just to say I love you, my darling husband."
Readers, I am a very humble person today. I have no reason
For anything in life; I just long for the lost love of my dear
Wife. I was out of town when my mother died. She died from a
Broken heart. Because my wife and I were out of town, she also
Died alone. So you see, my readers, I lost two loves in my life.
Luck has never been on my side. Why should
        it be, for I have SATAN?
I am one of a kind. You need to get to know me before I pass.
I may just live forever. Why not? I missed death eight times in
Life. Remember, my readers, all women are heroes here on earth.
Readers, love only gets stronger as the days and years go by.
A woman is to be loved—a real woman, that is. All women are
not the same, all people are not the same.
But most women need to be loved. True love to a man from a
Real woman only comes once in a lifetime. You will never get
That love back. How much does she mean to you in life?
For she is the biggest part of your life.
Sometimes I cry so much. I think there is a pond at the bottom
Of my feet that only comes from true love. You can't cry like
That over false love. True love can bring out that kind
Of true love from a person, for she was a special part of her
Man, as you were to her. Love will march on with time.
And at times, her love will still take your breath away,
For you will always be in love with that person in your life.
Even after death, love will always be in your heart,
And loneliness will keep trying to enter your mind.

But the upper hand is on your side,
For you now have good memory to fall back on each and every day
Of your life. Some of us may have no good memory or never had
A friend in life or wife. Now you are wide open for loneliness,
So you've always been a loner in life. When you are young, you
Feel you need no one in life but yourself. You are so very
Wrong. We all need someone, even more when you get up in age
And can no longer care for yourself. But there is always
Loneliness waiting for you. But never give up,
For there is always another way out. Just think about your
Past; there must be good things that you have done for yourself
Or perhaps a girlfriend that you may have liked
Or a pet. A pet can be a good friend in life.
For still waters run deep, for love is in the air.
Hello, it's me, my darling. I can hear you. I still say the wind
In the trees and the trees moving back and forth is my darling
Wife, saying hello to me the only way she can.
And it makes me feel so good and happy, for it only works
For me, for she was my lady in life, my woman, my wife,
And my lover. She was my other half in life.
She was my better half, I may add. Today my world is empty
Without her. So let her blow with the winds, move between the
Trees. I call up on her love for me to blow even harder.
I have so much to be thankful for in life. I had Regina
From the south, the love of my life. She has given me her
Whole love. At times I would cry, for there was too much love
At one time in my life. Can you believe that?
Why me? I would say. But I was in love with it all.
She could have done so much better in life than to pick me,
For she could have had the world. She gave it all up for me.
She was the entertainer of love, love that belongs to me.
She was the joy in my heart and soul.
Yes, she was the candle that kept the light burning in my heart.
Now the light is just about out, but the feeling is still
There. The feeling will never leave,
For she was my lady in life. Yes, I have walked with life,

But now I am ready to walk with death. All I ask is, please bring
Me home to my wife soon. We have been apart far too long.
It's time for me to come home.
At times I would throw a kiss to the winds and say goodbye.
Instead I threw a rope at a star and pulled her down to me
And planted that kiss on her lips and said, "I love you, my darling.
I love you. Please bring me home soon." Then I would remove
My rope and watch her slowly go home with a smile,
And a bright light was shining on me that put love
Back into my heart. She was the entertainer of my life STILL.
Readers, I just can't get enough of her love even after her death.
What does one do in life now? For there is no other,
Not in this world, for me.
She was put here only for me; I feel that in my heart and soul.
Speaking of soul, he, my soul, is still on that long trip, looking
For my wife. I may reach her before my soul comes to the
End of his trip. I have now moved to the other side
Of the railroad tracks, waiting for my train to heaven. I have
No place else to go, so I will just wait here for the rest of
My life for the train that's coming only for me.
But while I wait, I talk to you, my readers.
The love in my heart will go on after life with love
For her till the end of all times, for she does understand
That to be true. We are of one body still today.
Lord, where is my soul today? How many millions of miles have
He walked, still on the march, looking for my other half?
Bring me down a star, for my wife must be walking among them;
Let me reach out for a star and hold on to that promised
Land of dreams. Take me, dear, for I am yours. Take me from this
Old world into your new life,
For you can read my mind; you always could.
You know how I feel and what I must be thinking every day of
My life. I just want to leave Mr. Loneliness behind and Mr. Hate
To itself. I just want to bring all my love to you, my darling.
I reach out my arms to you. Come for me when you are ready,
But please make it sooner than later. At times I can smell

Your sweet love in the air, and I start to cry.
My heart starts to beat fast, then I must sit down for a minute.
I only wish I could have given you so much more in life, for
I am so sorry, darling. I know you said my love was more than
Any woman could ask for in life. You were just so kind to me.
You are a shining star in my life still today and always will
Be, till we meet in your world, darling. I go back in time
In my other two books, for we have walked many of miles in life.
My darling, one needs to read all three books to fully
Understand our way of life and the love we had for one another.
We are the last of the selfish ones, for we kept our love
To ourselves. What more could I ask for in life, for I had it
All. For I had you, my darling Regina from the south.
My wife, when we first met, opened up my
          heart, and she opened up the
Rest of my life. Every second in time is a chance for you
To hold the people that you love in life,
For my wife has been my inspiration for sixty years.
Readers, memories are like pictures in your mind, like the
Lovely smile she had and her beautiful black hair.
Memories are saying to me, it's a lonely day, and we need to take
Our walk along the path in the woods, where we can see the deer
Running up and down the hillside. For I have a library of books
In my memory bank, sixty good years of memories. My wife is in
Every page of that book of memories. For the library is the
Memory of the past, and each page sings a sweet song,
Stories that only she and I had experienced.
I loved her from the very first day we met at the beach, till
The day she passed in life some sixty years later.
How does one get over the love of an angel? She was the fire
In my heart and the light of my life.
But I have the library of books in my mind as you do, my readers,
For no one can open up our minds and take
          that from us, my readers.
That library will keep the door open to our hearts, my readers.
At times we must get off the path in life in order to see the light.

When it takes us nowhere in life, we then must take another
Path in life as I have done, for I stepped to the other side
Of the train tracks in order to see the train coming, not
Just to hear it pass me by. But now, to stop this train, for it
Will see me near the tracks and move on to the life with my wife
Right after death, I began to slip into darkness. And then, in
My ear, I heard a whisper, saying, "I have your back, my darling.
You won't slip anymore, for I am here.
For my love is always with you." At that moment, I felt so good.
I just wanted to cry, for time has gone by now. But I still
Long for her body at my side. I can feel my wife everywhere in
My heart. I can feel her when the wind blows
In the trees as they move from side to side.
Then that very warm feeling comes into my heart.
I will climb any mountain just to hold my wife for one moment
In time; all I need is just a moment.
To me, a moment would be a lifetime on earth. I would yell
From that mountaintop, "Darling, my love for you will
Overcome the distance between us,
For always, loving you is a must in this life and the next."
Regina, you are still the guiding light of my life.
Readers, if I was a duck,
I am not a drinking man, never had a drink in life. But if the
Ocean was made out of whiskey, I would dive to the bottom
And never come up.
Readers, Christmas is here once more. Loneliness will be
At its best. This is my third year alone.
I must go deep into my books of memory to keep out loneliness.
Readers, this is the time of the season. We need one another,
For I am here for you, my readers. My favor time in the year
Has always been Christmas. People seem to be in a better mood
When Christmas shows up once a year. Most people are happy.
Now take my lovely wife. Every day was Christmas to her as long
As she had me. That's what she tells me. In other words, all
Holidays were special to her, but she could take it or leave it.
And I loved her for that, for I must have Christmas. It is my

Time of the year. Look around you; most people are so happy.
Christmas is the month of our Lord. It is also the special
Month of my life. Now, most of my fire is out for Christmas.
Life is very uncertain for me today.
I just want to reach out into the universe, into darkness of
Love, till there is light beyond, the bewitch of darkness.
There is a whole new world out there for us after life here
On this earth, my readers.
Beyond the universe, there must be heaven, and there will be
My wife, Regina from the south,
Waiting for me and all of us, my readers.
          This is my way of thinking.
Readers, I will be working through some difficult decision.
I think I will move in with my son on the west coast.
I will make that long drive across county before Christmas.
All you need is a little hope. Hope I have; luck I don't have.
But Christmas is all about helping other people.
Most people today have forgotten about helping others.
Now it's only for themselves. Selfishness is not good anytime
Of the year. People will always need our love, for we must
Pull together in life. That's what it's all about, pulling
Together with love in our hearts.
We have the power to love. We were born with it.
Now I have given you the answer to love
And how to overtake loneliness and Mr. Hate,
For I am the gatekeeper to the trunk of this car.
This month is heart of the Christmas holidays.
This will be my last Christmas on the east coast. I am
A little sorry, for the east have been my home for eighty years.
And all my wife's dreams are here. Perhaps I may be back soon
If my train ride is late.
I have fallen in love with you, my readers, over the years.
I have never met any of you, but I can write to you, and
That was a happy time in my lovely life.
That was very big help to me just to have someone out there.
I can write to thank you, my readers. Perhaps one day, we will meet.

The world as of today belongs to people who hate. They have
No reason for it. They can't give you an answer why they hate.
Now I have the key to the trunk of the car Mr. Hate is driving.
When I open this trunk, will you listen to me this time?
For I have spoken to you over many years. No one listens
To me. Our time is running out on this planet.
When I put the key in the trunk and open it, I want to see
A big smile of love that will light up the trunk of that car,
And that will remove the hands of hate off the wheel and pull
Its foot from the gas pedal. And we will keep love behind the
Wheel of this car and run hate off the planet and take loneliness
With it.
Readers, as I said before, my book is all about loneliness
After the death of a loved one. This book is based on memory.
You must have memory to cope with being lonely and loneliness.
Loneliness can drive you mad over time. Take it from me.
I was just about there. I was for a while just about to go mad,
But I had no one to talk to me, like I am talking to you.
I know I go back in time in this book, but you need to
Understand how loneliness can work on the mind.
I will now continue with my story, readers. The power of love
Is the heart and soul of all beings. There is nothing we can't
Do in life with love in our hearts and soul, for I have
Walked the gates of hell with my wife's love in my heart and soul.
The power of her love was so great, not even the gates of hell
Could get to me. All I have is some heat marks on one of my
Legs, nothing more. Yes, my readers, I looked into the gates of hell,
And I saw fire. But the love of my wife had the power to
Pull me back into her world with the power of her love.
Everything I am telling you, my readers, took place in my life.
I have no reason to lie to you. It won't do me any good to lie.
I am from the old school. I tell it like I see it,
For I did not walk over a million miles doing sixty years to
Tell a LIE. I am for real, my readers. You can take that to the bank.
Now let's go on with our story.
Now I sit alone with loneliness, trying to sneak into my

Mind, but I have too many good memories that will give me a full
Mind of good things in the past. Yes, like all of us,
At times we fall back a little, and here comes guess who, loneliness.
But, readers, we now know how to push loneliness aside.
Memories, we all have some good memory in life.
Call on those memories to keep you happy,
For we all at one time or another must have loved someone in life.
Could be just a friend or even a pet,
Nothing in life's gonna change my love in life for my darling
Wife, who is no longer with me. She left me with a million
Years of memories with love. The beat of my heart is like a
Locomotive running downhill in full speed, looking for the
Lost love I once had, for the power of true love will never die.
The heart, over time, may slow to a beat, but the soul will love
On long after life on this earth. As I said, the heart may slow
Down, but the beat will still be there.
Readers, cherish the loved ones in your life, for life on this
Earth for us today is only a footstep in time, so please
Cherish your loved ones in life, for tomorrow could be a step
Too late. My dear wife and I had all the love two people needed
On this earth, but we were two black people on this plane,
Trying to make it in life. We had to fight hate every day we
Open our doors, but we had true love. Not even hate could come
Between us. But easy, it was not.
We were the rulers in our own hearts and life,
Not hate from anyone. We must stay strong. We must keep love in
Our hearts. Let Mr. Hate realize that we have all powers of love,
Front and center in our hearts. It a very cold night.
The winds are blowing by my ears. Could it be my wife?
The trees are also blowing. Will I receive a wisp of her voice?
Will the trees wrap around me and say, "Darling, it's me, only for a
Moment, for I will blow by from time to time. This is only
Between you and I, my darling, for no one else would
Believe this, and that's okay too, my darling, for I
Belong only to you, not the rest of the world.
If you should need me, just call me, for I am in the trees.

The winds and the stars, my love, is all around you, my darling."
Readers, I had a weak moment late in the night.
I was like a mad wolf in the woods. I got up out of my chair
In the living room, where I sit and sleep most of my life away.
I just walk from room to room. I had the hunger for my wife's love.
The desire was so great. At times, I seem like a wild man.
This went on for more than two hours.
I was hungry for the love of my wife, Regina.
For a moment, I felt like a bestial person, AN animal,
Then I got a hold of myself and took a seat in my chair.
I then could feel something near to me, so I looked over my
Right, and with a smile, there was Mr. Loneliness. It said, "I am
Always here for you when you have a weak moment, and then I will
Move in." He said, "It was me who took you on that two-hour walk.
It was me, who just about made you go mad.
        But you were too strong
For me, but there will be another time." Readers, it will never
End, but we must keep an open mind, your memory. I forgot
For a while, for it only takes a moment to leave yourself open.
I pledge my love, and all my love, to my darling wife
Throughout endless times. Precious moments
        we once had in life will
Die with me, for they were our moments,
Who once said back in time, give me life or give me death.
But I say to you, my readers, give me death and take me to my
Wife, for I no longer wish to live alone.
For we had so many sentimental reasons to love, just to kiss
And hold hands. That's only as we, true lovers, could understand.
At times it felt like we would trade our hearts from body to one
Body, for the love was so good and pure. Neither one of
Us at times could hold back the tears of our love for one another.
We would just hold each other and cry for a moment of true
Love, then we would kiss. My wife's voice mail is still in
Her cell phone. So I called her the other day. Her sweet
Voice came over the phone, "I am not at my phone
Now, but place your message, and I will soon get back to you."

How would that make you feel, my readers? How would that make
You feel once more? The message I left, for I only had a moment,
"I love you, my darling. Please come for me, for I long for your
Love. Bring me home." Then I went offline, and the phone went
Dead. So, my readers, I wait. All I have is time. My train
Ride should be coming soon. I can never take her voice out
Of her cell phone. That lovely voice is so real to me.
I kiss the phone and hope to feel her lips.
I am a man from the dark side of life. She was an angel of light.
Together we were the powerhouse of love, for we had each other.
No human on this earth could bring us down.
Yes, I want to be on your everyday list in life and after life,
For I say, give lasting death or give me Regina.
My lost soul should be near, dear, for it had
         been gone for more than
Two years. Keep an eye out for it, my darling,
For I hope to be on that train soon to you, my darling,
For I am now on the right side of track.
So I wait for that phone call, telling me that she got
My message and will get back to me soon.
So, my readers, I wait, and I wait.
As I stay on the path to everlasting life,
I received a voice mail on my phone ten days after I called my
Wife on her voice mail and left a message. The voice message
On my phone was, "Kenny, Kenny." Over the years, she would call
Me Kenny a few times.
That voice on my phone was very soft and sweet.
Am I losing my mind? Perhaps. I will accept anything today.
That brings me closer to my wife. Was that her on the phone?
Perhaps not. But we don't know for sure, do we?
But it gave me hope. I have nothing else in life.
I will accept her anyway she comes to me after life,
For now my world is upside down. Seems like everything in
My life is wrong today.
Readers, I may die in this chair in my living room,
For I really don't care anymore. Yes, I have my son, and he

Needs me as I do him, but the love of my life is gone.
So are all my hopes and dreams are gone with my wife.
I have no one to come home to or to leave home for.
After sixty years of coming home to the woman you loved,
Guess who is waiting for you at home now?
Loneliness. And it wants to take the place of your wife,
Your wife of sixty years. I won't stand for it, my readers.
I will fight loneliness for every moment in each hour of the
Day and night. It will never take the place of my wife.
Readers, we now know all about memories, and that will give
Us a full mind of love and peace.
My life now is like a long and lonely road, where I will keep
My heart out front, and we will walk this road together
While I wait for my train to come down to me.
I just may run into my long-lost soul, for it has been gone
For just about two years now. For my darling wife's death has been
Well over two years now.
All I long for now is peace in my heart, and that will be hard to
Find in this world today, There is far too much hate in this world
Today. There is no real understanding of one another in
This world today. Understanding and love seem to be a
Thing of the past, for the good ship in the human life have sailed.
Remember, back in time, I was telling you about the storm that was
Coming. Well, it's still coming. The next big rain, you see,
May just be that storm of all times. Hate on this planet
Will bring on this everlasting storm,
For I don't mean to scare or frighten you, but that storm is coming.
We must have more love in life, people.
We just can't stand aside anymore and let hate run over us,
For we have the power of love, so let's put a stop to all of this.
At my age, my days are about over. But for you, young people,
This is your time in life. Make a stand for peace and for love.
I can only tell you what's coming,
For I have been there. I have the wounds and pain all over my
Body and mind.
My story is true in my heart and soul, for my wife and I both

Have been there. We walked many of hard roads. This I hope
You will never need to do in life. This is why I am telling
You my story. The thing is, will you listen?
Perhaps we need to sing more love songs instead of yelling
Hate words at one another. I keep going back in time,
Telling you about this storm. But over the years, no one's listening
To me. Just look at your TV, open your front door, and look
Out into the streets. What do you see? Killing everywhere.
You're not even safe in your own homes today. Why is this in one
Word, HATE?
How does one give your life more meaning, finding
The true love of your life? And that may take the rest of your
Life, or it may take just a moment. As for me, it took only a
Moment in time. Remember, my readers, love is a two-way street.
My readers, we were all given the great power of love.
But there is so much evil and wickedness in this world.
Today it has become very hard to keep love alive.
In a way, I feel sorry for us, as people on this earth,
For the world once belonged to all of us,
But now the new rule is power and money.
Don't forget greed. But we still act like everything is okay.
Today, this is what hate and loneliness can do to a mind.
Readers, I am just an everyday guy. Most people don't know me or
May not want to know me. People, that may be some kind of a joke.
But my readers should know me by now,
        for most of you, my readers,
Have been with me for more than sixty years.
Readers, have you really loved a woman like I have?
You need to go deep inside her heart, feel her feeling,
Learn all her thoughts, understand her true feeling,
Then you may be halfway to her heart.
It takes time. You can fall in love in a minute,
But it takes years for two people to become one. Once you both
Reach that point in life, no one can ever take that from you.
Love is then till death do you part. Your love will then
Run with you throughout time.

What can we do to keep love in the driver's seat? A smile would
Help open a door for someone, anyone.
Just reach out to another human with love would put love
Front and center. It will take time to overcome hate,
For this was not an overnight thing. This was growing over
The years. For we can still pull love back into all of our
Hearts. For we must pull together, not apart.
After my wife's death, I have eaten so many TV dinners.
I hate to cook for just myself. All the fun is now gone from
Cooking. I loved to cook for my wife. But today, it's TV dinner
For myself, and I hate TV dinners. But this is my
Way of life today.
Readers, I jump around in my book, for life will never take
A straight road. So I keep going back in time in my
Book, my wife and I, who are two black people in this world.
Like most black people, times were and still are very
Hard today. Memories are all over the sixty years of love
That my wife and I had together. Today, memories are the
Keys to my story. Remember, my readers, as you read on
With my story, memory is the key to this story.
Memory is the key to loneliness.
As I once said to you before, a writer I am not. Don't wish to
Be a writer. Something made me take a PEN and tell you my story.
This goes beyond the limits of whether you believe this story.
My feeling and my soul stand with the truth.
Every word in my story is true. Before I leave this world, I want
You to know the truth. It will open some big doors in life
For us as black people. My experience is gold,
For you can't find this in any other bookstore.
There are no records in this world about my experience.
Only I can tell this story, for it is now my life.
Remember the grave that I fell into as a kid and Satan on
My chest, and I walked up to the gates of hell twice.
When the angel was put out of heaven and on his way down,
He passed me by inches, close enough to reach out for me
While I was standing in that open grave at midnight.

Later in my life, I was hit by lightning twice. I was out for
Two days. This may be hard for you to believe, not when Satan
Is still at your side, and there is nothing you can do about it.
A large piece of equipment rolled over on me three times in life,
But I am still here. My doctor said, "Why are you still here?"
And the question is, Why am I still here?
Perhaps to tell you my story. I'd been to hell and back twice.
Is that not a story to tell? Will you listen and understand?
That is the real question. For sometimes the truth hurts.
I have given you an open door to the future for a black man
In this world. I have also given you the answer to loneliness.
In life, memory is the key to loneliness.
I know it may be hard for you to believe my story, but do
You know of anyone else on this earth who has been with Satan
Twice in life? And there is nothing I can do about it.
My story may be a little more than some of you can handle,
And that would be understandable. Let me say to you,
I don't drink, nor do I smoke, and I don't take drugs.
I am just a straight-up guy who was in the wrong place at
The wrong time. I've only been to church twice in life.
I would go to church every day if it would get Satan off my
Back. But church won't help me now, for it is too late for me in
Life. I am a straight person. I keep telling you in my story
That everything is true.
There is no living person who can tell you this story
But me. If you don't believe this story, then it is
Truly your great loss, for I don't know what else to tell you.
You have my full story.
When I would kiss my wife's lips, my heart would beat twice as
Fast. The birds over my head would sing a love song,
And the sky would be bright blue, with love running down on me.
She was my everything, for I needed her close to my heart every
Day of the week. For I had the world in my hands, for I
Had her love in my heart. The world at times seems like a little
Ball in my hands, and I dance all around it with the love of
Regina in my heart. My heart seems big as the ball in my hand.

I knew then, it was too late to even turn back now,
For I was deeply in love, perhaps over my head. Then let
Me drown with all this love. Death passed me by seven times in
Life. It was love that overpowered death. Look at me. Explain
Why I am still here. True love can overcome death at times.
The death of my wife was the cause of human beginning and Satan.
She was passed from hospital to hospital within three states.
They just let her die. It hurts me so much to talk about the
Death of my wife.
Today I stand in the shadows of love, for good things don't
Last forever. Only bad dreams seem to last forever.
Love is the sweetest thing in life. It takes over your heart
And soul. You will then feel happiness and everlasting joy.
Take it from me, for I know. Today this old heart of mine can't
Hold on for too much longer. I do look for the promised
Land of life thereafter. I need to rest. I only sleep two hours
Per night. I just want to lie down and sleep and reach out
For my dear wife, Regina. I long for that journey,
For I have lived in two worlds, the world before your time
And the world today. My wife was never in the old world.
I had to pass over into the new world to meet her.
It was well worth the trip. I just wish I could have met
Her back in time, my world. She would have been a great queen
Of my world. We would have ruled together. Her beauty would
Have put her out front of all other queens in the old world
That I once knew. Her IQ would have been received as magnificent.
Back in the old world, she would have been my queen.
Yes, we would have been king and queen.
Most readers today will never understand the love we had for
One another. This is only one in a million.
Love does come along at first sight back in the day when we
First met early years. Yes, you could fall in love at
First sight, for I did. This is a new day. Things are not the
Same. Today is all about MONEY, POWER, GREED, AND HATE.
So where is love today? I can tell you this: it's not first
Sight or front and center. If you have real love today,

You are one in a million, a very lucky person.
Because you can't buy real love. It's not for sale. That is not
Real love. Real, true love can stop all pain and hate.
Take it from me; I know. REMEMBER, I've
        been to the gates of hell twice,
Had Satan to seat on my chest, but the love of my wife kept
Me around. Love will always be the key word in life, people.
I had many misty blue days and nights, and there was no one
For me to call on for help. Yes, I have a son, and I love him,
But he is not my loving wife. He can't give me the power of love,
Like my wife could. She would walk off the edge for me.
She would even give up her life for me if need be.
And I would do the same for her. How many people do you know
Would do that for you? It was called real love back in the day,
When it was the good old days for some of us.
My race, the black race, live for love and our women.
We have very little money, but we have love for our women.
We would go to hell and back for our women. Would you, white
People? PERHAPS. Then perhaps for money and power only,
But not for one's soul. But I would, for the soul of my woman.
There will never be real peace on this earth, not today anyway.
Between all the people, we must do a better job and get along.
We must stop this hate and kill the storm that's coming for us.
This we must stop now, for we are running out of time.
I won't say this to you anymore, or perhaps maybe a few
More times in my story, just to be sure you get the true picture.
For later, there may be no time to tell.
This is the last of the three-part story of my book,
The love of my wife and I had for one another.
Then there is the evil hate that is running wild today
When I was at the age of TEN, as I said to you so many times
In my story. I just don't want you
To forget that I fell into that open grave. From that day
Till today, my life has been hell, for Satan is still with me.
And now, without my wife, I could be in trouble.
I loved my wife yesterday, and I love her even more today.

And I will love her throughout time. There is no bottom
To the love I have for my wife. You need to find another
Word for deep love, for I have ran past deep love down to my
Lost soul.
Readers, today, as I write, Christmas is near, the worst time
Of the year to be lonely. We all love Christmas, most of us
Anyway. And so does loneliness. Loneliness is very big on
Christmas, for our hearts are very weak at that time of year.
So, my readers, hold on tight to all your memories, for we are
Going to need them. For our memory must be front and center
At Christmas. We all will need a little help over Christmas.
We, with our memory, will keep loneliness afar.
Readers, as today I write the last of my story, this is the
Month of December, Christmas month. Another lonely year has
Gone by in life for me alone. It is my third year without
My wife.
But I have you, my readers. I would have
        been lost alone without your
Help, my faithful readers,
Just between you and me, my readers. I am getting
Too old to write. My eyes are not what they once were,
Plus I hate to write. Over the years, I would hate to write my
Own name. My wife would do it for me. Now I am writing a book,
The story of my wife and myself that's hard for me to take in.
But this story MUST BE TOLD, for Satan is still in my back
Pocket. And there is nothing I can do about it but to tell my
Story, for you, as my readers, will know all about the evil we live
Within life, mainly me, my readers.
Readers, the nights and days seem like they are forever
Without my wife.
Now, readers, let me back up in time a few years, like forty.
If you have not read the first volume of my book,
Then you should. It will bring you up-to-date with the second
Volume. Let me refresh back just a little for you.
I have used up six ballpoint pens because the ink would become
Warm and leak over the paper. I have never seen anything

Like that in my life. Could that be just a bad set of pens?
I don't think so. Why should I think this way?
Because of all the evil things that had taken place in my life.
Evil things do happen in life, my life for sure.
This you and I know. You would know if you have read the first
Volume. There is an evil that doesn't want me to tell you my life
Story. I will buy a million pens if need be to write our story.
No one or nothing will stop my life story.
I am a lonely soul, but my heart is full of love due to my dear
Wife when she was on this earth only a few short moments.
She also wants me to tell you our story of life.
Readers, you need to know. The world needs to know. And I must
Tell it all today, for it will make me feel better once I
Leave this earth, looking for my wife.
For Satan has been a very large part of my life,
All due to the fact I fell in that open grave at the cemetery
On that cold and very dark night. I was a boy of the age ten.
Since then, nothing's been the same for my wife and I.
I see that bad things in life are not done with me yet.
That's okay because I am alone today, and he can't hurt my wife
Anymore. All this is very real, my friends. I know it's hard
To believe, but have you ever been to the dark side of life?
I mean, to the front gates of hell. Believe me, it's no fun.
Then forty years later, here is Satan, sitting on my chest.
Call me mad. I can tell you this: I should be mad. Thanks
To my wife, I am not mad. I am in love with her power of love.
Many times, she has overruled Satan. That's another reason why
She is no longer with me today. But I should not be here today.
Death passed me up seven times in life, but it took my wife
The first time around. Readers, it will be a sad day if you don't
Believe in me, for then, Satan would have won because you,
The people, think he's not real. That just gives him more power
On this earth to do as he pleases, for he is now bringing
The great storm. You do remember the storm, for it's still coming.
Readers, my journey in time has not been a good one for me or
My dear wife. Readers, you have known me and my wife since

My birth. We should be good friends by now.
Readers, perhaps someday we must meet at the good will dressure
Draw SMILE, about seventy-eight years ago. We were both very
Young, and most of us have grown old over the years together.
A lot have taken place in our lives over seventy-five when
She passed away, and I was then alone. I had three years on her
In age. Readers, many times over the years, I asked you if you would
Want to walk in my shoes just for a day,
Just for one day on planet earth. That will be the day you will
Never forget, and to make matters worse, just being a black man
With Satan now on your back for seventy-eight years.
What would one say about that? Now you have more than the world
On your back, for there is Satan.
When I was ten years old, I was in the wrong place at the wrong
Time or, should I say, the wrong grave. All he wanted was my soul.
But someone said no to him and to be on your way.
But he's been on my back for seventy-eight years,
A day in the life of a black man. On that day, at the grave, my
Soul was out of his reach. So over the years, he found a way to
Take my dear wife. He gave her nothing but pain for three months,
Not even the doctors could stop the pain. They said to me,
"We don't understand any of this." But, readers, I understood.
It was me who he wanted. Killing my wife with pain was just
To upset me. And he got his wish. I am now a shell of a man.
But she went to her Lord. She had a good soul and loved her
LORD. She was taken into heaven, and that made me so pleased.
So, readers, here I am alone, just him and I.
I look forward to the day we meet, for we have had this feud
For sixty-eight years. Now that my wife is gone, I really don't
Care anymore about myself. So I wait every day, and I will
See what takes place next. IT'S his move.
Readers, this is like a runaway truck coming down the
Highway behind you. By the time you turn around, it's too late.
Perhaps the whole idea is too much for you, my readers.
The storm. Satan. Hate. Evil. This is so much for anyone to
Receive at one time in life. But, people, we are out of time.

I am giving you a heads-up. You can look this straight in the eye
And put hate to rest, only if we pull together now, not later.
People, hate is everywhere today. In your homes. In the stress.
At work. We must put a stop to this hate. My wife would want
This people, less so it for her, for she loved you as people
Of this planet. People, we need to do a swift rotation from hate
To love. I know you can do this. We were not born with hate
In our hearts but with love. Somehow along the way, we lost
Our love for one another. Now it's time to regain possession
Of our love and faith in one another.
Readers, I have difficult times now, trying to keep myself
Together. I feel like a shell of once was a man and a king
Now sitting along the beach, waiting for a wave of water
To come and take me out to sea.
I more or less have tunnel, my way through life the hard way.
I have given it my all and then some,
Maximum performance as a black man, and still came up short.
One could call it many roadblocks. My real pleasure and
Enjoyment and satisfaction were my wife's true love from the heart.
She was my hopes and dreams. At the end of every day, I had her
To come home to. Now that is gone. So are my hopes and dreams.
She was like a flower that never dies, a dream that only
Most men could wish for in life. To me she was one of God's angels.
That was sent to me to keep me on track.
When I was a very young, black man, I would go off to myself
And wish for a woman like I once had.
She came to me when I was heartbroken. At that time in my life,
I was down and out. I was at the beach, walking alone, then
Along came this beautiful light, the light of my life.
I knew, from that moment, she had to be my wife in life.
She must be my lady of love in life for me and only me.
My heart was beating so hard that I had chest pains.
I was at that point, just a little weak. Her eyes were
Like a star in the sky. I could see myself in her eyes.
I still have clear vision today about my past life.
I can see wars, myself as the black king, me going to war.

The dream only lasts for a moment. At any time, I can get
Flashbacks, and it's all so clear and real. I can see
Blood. I can feel the pain in those moments.
When I die, I may go back to my past life as a king
With my wife at my side. Readers, I hope not for I have seen
Too many wars, I just want to walk along the stars with my wife.
Readers, you have given me hope in life, for I hope someone
Is reading our life story. I want my dear wife's death to leave
A song in this world. To me she was a symbol of life.
I just want the world to understand the
          kind of woman my wife was.
She was not just my wife; she was an angel on earth.
She was an angel of the world. Anyone that knew her would
Say she was an angel. You need to look outside of the
Box to understand what I am saying to you, readers.
She was a perfect catch. How often do you catch an angel on
Earth?
Readers, you may take notice, I keep going back in time.
This needs to be done to keep us front and center.
I move around in history. Readers, it's getting so painful to
Watch TV anymore, especially for the black race.
We are a peaceful race of people.
Readers, let me ask you, who marched on the Capitol building in
2020? Not the black people. Need I say anymore?
I could say a lot, but that won't help matters any.
One would say, why should we listen to
          him? That's a good question.
Once more, let's try and tell you why for the third time.
I can see a rainy day coming, rain like we've never seen before,
Then behind that, this big storm that will take up the whole sky.
I don't wish to scare anyone, but you better wake up.
My sense of sight today is unusual. The vision I have today
Comes from a lot of things, and most of those things are bad,
Like the sense of cold evil when I was in that grave
Or two trips to the front gates of hell
Or Satan sitting on my chest. People, life has been hell for me.

The only faith and hope I had was my wife. Now that she is
No longer here, I am lost. Most of the time, I can't tell you
What day of the week it is. But in the back of my mind,
Every day I can see this storm coming. To me it is very clear.
He never spoke one word, just looked into my eyes.
From that I can see things to come, like this storm of hate.
And we, the people, cause this to happen. We fell in love with
The word HATE. Now it's running wild.
Somewhere out there, it must be an answer to all our hate for
One another. We need to find that answer and fast.
I could very easily sit on the sidelines and say nothing
About the storm, and all the hate is going on today.
Sit at home, and watch people kill one another.
Just look at the TV, and all the action is right in front of you.
But my wife and I are not that kind of people. What more
Do I want you to know? I once loved this old world,
Till hate took over. Seems like there is a race war, been the
People of all colors now. At first, it was just black and
White. Now it has run over to all the dark colors.
The only ones who can walk around free today and not worry about
Getting killed are the white people.
Something is very wrong with this picture.
Readers, I need my Goodwill dresser drawer before the great storm
Comes. Perhaps I can go back in time and seek refuge by
Hiding in that Goodwill dresser drawer.
I would try anything to hide from this storm.
But there is no hiding from this storm. This will be the storm
Of all storms, years of hate and evil pulling together
To overrun the earth with hate.
Readers, this will be my last book on the east coast.
I am moving west with son in December of this year.
Three years alone is just a little too much,
For I find I am talking to myself. I even talk to loneliness.
That's when I said to myself, it's time to move west with my son,
This is the third book in my life.
All three volumes run together, from childbirth till

The age of eighty, to understand the life of mine and my wife.
One must read all three volumes; it's all one story.
I must keep going back in time, my readers, for this is my life.
Our lives are in all three books. These books are one in a million.
There will never be another Ken Murrey in life; that would be me.
Who else do you know had been to the gates of hell twice
And had Satan sit on his chest?
I guess one could say I am Satan's boy. I am not pleased about it
At all, but there is nothing I can do about it.
But for how long, I don't know. Maybe till death do us part.
And the angel and queen Regina will be no more on this earth.
She was one of the Lord's special people, and she was sent here
For me. MEMORY, I have sixty years of good memory.
After you have lost a loved one in life, there will always be
Good memory; that's why I must keep going back in time, MEMORY.
Take me all over the world of having good times with my wife.
As you read my book, you may say to yourself, I have seen this
Line before. Of course you have, for time takes me back and
Forth. At times I have no control of my mind.
I can still see my grandfather working seven days a week
For seventy years on a farm at forty dollars per week,
Seven days a week, from sunup till sundown, with no fault
Of his own, for he was just a poor black man, trying to make
A living for his family.
But, readers, in my mind, I have memory of his life.
None of it was good. All he knew was work and more work.
That's all it was back in the day for a black man,
Not much better today. But once more, it's about memory,
For my mind works around the clock.
Readers, love and memories are the key to life, even more so
After you have lost a loved one in life.
I have one last bell to answer to in life, the bell of that
Train that will be coming for me very soon, I hope.
For I am standing now on the train track, waiting for my ride
To my wife, for she has stayed in my corner for more than
Sixty tears. So I know, after death, she will never let me

Down, even after death. Our souls are still together. All those,
My soul has been on a hunt for three years now, looking
For my wife. I wish it all the luck.
Readers, I need a gift card to heaven, for I need a miracle
On a supernatural train ride.
Readers, the very first time I've ever seen my wife's face was on
A hot beach in Maryland. From that day till today, love was all
Over me. Readers, I want to go home. I want to go home this
Year. That's my wish for Christmas to myself.
I wish to catch up with my long-lost soul and travel that long
Road home with him. We will walk with time till we reach the
Light at the end or our road.
Ask the lonely how they feel. Ask me, for I can tell you how lonely it
Feels. From this moment in time, where has all my love gone?
Where is the real love I once had in life?
Life is so unfair, for I could never fall in love with someone
Else, NEVER could I fall in love with another.
I am a one-woman lover, for I have given her all my love for
The hereafter. The spring have gone from my heart,
But, my readers, I can still dream. It is painful at times,
But it feels so good. The walks we once took
And the love song she would sing to me and that lovely smile
She had would drop you to your knees. My God, she was so lovely.
Regina, my darling, when I reach you, I'm gonna love you just a
Little more, if that's even possible, my dear.
What was so easy for two is so hard for one. I can't seem to
Do anything without you. Perhaps I don't
        wish to be alone. That's what
Make it so hard, for I was born to love only Regina in life.
My body has an age number. My soul would be eighty.
My heart will run with time, so there is no number for the heart.
It is endless in time. The love of the heart will never run out.
When we were very young in life, we made a promise to each
Other that we will always love one another throughout time.
She is no longer with me today, but that promise is still very
Real. Her lovely spirit and feelings are all around me.

I can still feel her love throughout my body.
Only true love will maintain in your body for a lifetime.
We call that old-school love. Most young people will
Know nothing of that. I mean, there is love, then there is real
Love to die for.
Readers, should I say more, for I loved that wife of mine.
I love her even more after death, and I will love her till
The end of time. And time will never run out.
Call me sentimental, but I am in love throughout time, for she
Is there.

THIS IS AN INTERMISSION PERIOD BETWEEN NOW AND THEN

Readers, let me run offtrack for just a moment, back about
Fifty years.
I just want to go way back in time.
I was in my teens. Things where very hard for me as a black
Person, just a little history of my life before I met my wife.
Bad things went on for the black man. They are still very
Much here today, perhaps not as hard but very much here.
Sorry to have gotten offtrack, but these are things
You should know. But this was a very large part of my life.
Then along came Satan, when I was only at the age of TEN.
OKAY, let me get back on track.

This is a new world. Things are moving so fast today.
Even time will be out of your reach if you don't look
Ahead and make your move. We, as a people, black
People, need to pull together. We are god people,
We must be number one in the eyes of the Lord
For all the hell we have taken. No one could have
Overcome but the chosen ones of God.
I know we are the chosen ones. Look at me.
Am I not writing my story? I am still here today.
Don't misunderstand me. I love all human beings,
Just don't trust the white men. Why should I
Trust them? Would you trust them? Always keep the ones
You don't trust in front of you,
And keep an open mind. Just be yourself, and you will
Always be on the right path in life.
You can always step off in life for a break
And look things over. Never run down a blind road when
You can walk. You may want to think about this
Road in life and back up for a second or two.
Rethink. You can't go wrong. Your life belongs to you,
Only you. You alone control your own life.
For me, at early times in life, I was only ten years old,
I knew none of what I know today. I am very sorry for that.
Things that happen to me in life, I believe, is not a mistake,
All part of when I was a kid and fell in that open grave
At midnight. I was only ten years old
When that cold hand reached out for me in that moment of time.
Evil will be with me throughout my life.
With me, evil can't win, for there is a higher hand
On my soul and heart, for my God is my keeper.
If not, I would have been taken when I was only ten years old.

This is one black man that will walk the path to heaven.
Readers, it is a beautiful world, and it is waiting for you.
Only people become ugly, and unsightly things can and will
Become unfair in life. But that, people, you need to deal
With as you pass through life. White people know and knew
For years, back when we were slaves. We must keep the black
Man down, if he ever gets a foothold. There is no stopping
As a man. Today we have a foothold, and we are off and running.
Education and knowledge are the key to put us on top.
Education will give you the key to our future,
The period of time yet to be for us as a black man.
Never give up. Never stop pushing for a better life, for you
Are all that you wish to be and more.
When I was growing up, I had no father.
          My mother was a beautiful
Young woman. She had many jobs and young men.
I was lucky to see her once a week.
She did what she could to keep food on the table.
But there were four of us, more or less.
I left home at the age of ten. I was just a kid.
I would wash cars for money, cut lawns for white people.
Black people had no lawns to cut or had no money.
I would push snow for white people, take out trash for white people.
I could go on and on. I knew what a dollar could do for me,
Put food in my stomach. I slept under a bridge most of my
Young life. I went home at times to check on my two brothers
And one sister. My mother was never at home;
At work, I like to think. At ten, I fell in love with the library
Books. I read everything outside of the bridge. The library
Was my second home, plus it kept me out of the weather.
I put myself through school by library books. Perhaps I mentioned
This to you before. At my age, I forget at times, so I tell
It to you once more, plus you need to hear it a second time.
Like I said to you some years back, I have six trades,
All licenses in my name. Let me tell you more of my story
When I was very young, when I had my business before I

Got sick and lost everything. I was in construction business.
One day, while cutting a field, the owner came to me and said,
"I want to put in a pond right here, where we are standing,
For my horses. Have you ever done anything like a pond?"
Now I gave him credit for even asking a black man.
This job calls for an engineer, and we know I am not
An engineer, but I am the best of whatever I do. Things just
Come to me at will. So my answer to the owner, "Yes, I can put
In a pond for you." His answer, "Good. Give me a week to lay it
Out on paper, and you can take it from there." "Okay," I said.
Then I said to myself, "Am I in over my head?" Well, I've been
Over my head many times before. For a black man to make it,
You must go big, take that chance. I went to the library and
Read many books on putting in a pond. Two weeks went by; I
Received a call. "When can you start my pond?"
My answer was first of the month, ten days from now.
I lost many nights of sleep just thinking about this pond.
First day of the pond, my backhoe and I started in the center
Of that circle, which will become a pond.
There was a springhouse twenty-five feet from where the
Pond would be dug. I ran a line from the springhouse to
The pond. As the pond filled up to a level, there was another
Line on the other side of that pond where the water would
Run out without overrunning the pond.
Before the water entered the pond,
I put one hundred tons of crushed stone.
        This would help to keep the
Water level.
Ten days from start to finish, the pond was finished.
Word got out. Look at this beautiful pond? It was in all the
Papers. Most people had a very hard time believing that this
Was done by a black man, myself. Respect was very high that
Day. I had flowers all around the pond. It was and still is one
Of the most beautiful ponds that I have ever seen.
I was the builder, but to this day, they can't understand how
A black man can do a job of this beauty.

All that to say to you, the black men, there is nothing you can't
Do. Back in the day, the white man walked on one side of
The street and the black man on the other side.
Today we both are on the same side of the street. Things are
A little better. We all know a little more now.
When I die and go to heaven, I will put in a special request
For Jim Crow to be sent straight to hell. I personally
Know the headman in hell,
Black man. For me, it has been a very long ride,
But things will be better for you the next generation.
There are many doors for you, the black man, that can be opened.
Today, reach high, never go for less.
You are better than most men. You are a black man.
I feel, as a black person, the best of my life is yet to
Come. There must be a better life for me and my wife.
I refuse to die and take hell with me. As my readers, I want
The world to know what hell is all about.
Living, for a black person, is hell on this planet, but the
Dark side of life is a whole new world. I have visited that
World twice. The only difference is, there are no white or black;
We are all the same. As a people, we need each other while we
Are still living. But most of us don't realize that
Some of us think we are better than others.
That alone is a living hell for the black race. But the day
Is coming, and it is so very near. And at that time, it will
Be too late to say "I am sorry." We are all brothers and sisters.
We are all one race of human being.
You may not like it, but we are here together.
I feel sorry for the human race for what we have become.
So, readers, stand tall and keep the faith.
Walk with me and the human race to a new start in life.
We can live together; we must, as people.
It has not been easy for me telling my story.
There is a path of light for each one of us after death.
If there is a heaven for us, we must do right here on earth.
The old saying is, you were born with a black soul.

No human was born with a black soul,
But evil is everywhere. It can and will take over your way
Of thinking, and it has done just that over many years.
We need to overcome by reaching out to each other.
If not, then we all will see each other in hell,
Then there is no coming back for a second chance at life.
We gave that up to be number one.
I believe with all my heart, when I was a kid and fell in
That open grave at midnight, at the same time, an angel was
Kicked out of heaven and fell close enough to me to reach
Out and put a hand on my body on his way down
To reach for a human soul, to get even with the Lord.
Why else could I have come face-to-face with him in life
And then stood at the gates of hell? But I am still here today.
My Lord also has a hand on me. We won't go without
A fight. I believe in the Lord;
I believe in me as a human being. I believe in me,
And I believe in life. I am not a man of the clork, nor do
I wear a garment. I've only been to church twice in my life,
But I am the only living soul that can tell this story.
You will never ever hear it from another human being.
I was the only one in that grave on that special night when
The angel was put out of heaven and came from inches of
Passing me. Only I have the right to tell this story,
And I am giving it to you.
I want the next generation of colored people,
Especially black men, to know that the world is waiting
For you. You were born with what it takes to be a leader.
You are a winner. Let no one tell you any different.
You can be successful in anything,
Whatever you wish to do in life. In my heart, I have shared
Some of my hard-earned lessons that I am still living
With each and every day of my life.
I trust that you will find your own path in life.
The world is waiting for you
With all it's good and bad. But you, as a black man, have what it

Takes to overcome. You were born with a gift.
Look at me. Lesson one: I am still here. I have beaten the worst
Of the dark side; I have taken everything the white man
Has thrown at me. Remember, he is only a man, a human being
Like yourself. He can never take your heart or soul.
He can slow you down but never stop you in life,
Now, on the other hand, the dark side is a whole new
Story. It is not a man, not human.
It is evil. It can take your heart and soul. The white man
Is only a kindergarten joke compared to the dark side,
I've been there twice in my life. I don't think you will ever
Need to worry about the dark side. I was just in the wrong
Grave at the wrong moment in time. It took a brief of a second
For me to meet the dark side of life. I embark on telling
You my story of life because my life story was hell.
There is no need for you, the next generation, to ever
Experience my side of life. Today is a new world for this
Next generation.
Today was sunny, so I got out of my chair and went for a walk
With her cell phone in my pocket.
All that day, I had a lovely, warm feeling in my pocket.
I walked all that day, and I felt very good.
That was the first since her death.
But now I can carry her voice around with me.
That has given me just a little hope in life, for she is still
Here at my side. I can climb that mountain now. There is hope
For me now in her love, the power of MEMORIES.
She wants me to have her cell phone, and I keep it fully charged.
For it stayed on full charge for a full year on its own,
And it was overlooked by her sisters when they were cleaning
Out her dresser after she passed.
Perhaps, my readers, when they cleaned out
        the dresser, that cell phone
Was not there. Remember now, readers, back seventy-eight years
Ago. I was born in that Goodwill dresser drawer,
And I would tell that story to my wife many times over the years.

Can it be that the two dressers came together? Can it be
My wife did this because I was born in a dresser drawer?
Readers, what better place to put her spirit but into
Her cell phone, with her sweet voice that I so loved, then on
Her cell phone that I could listen to day and night.
She knew I would understand. Yes, my wife
          is back with me through
Her voice mail. She has given me this cell phone to ease the
Pain in my heart, and I will call on it through my time on
This earth.
Readers, that cell phone just put loneliness out of business.
It was overruled by a cell phone that was full of love for me.
Just her sweet voice was the voice of true love.
I only wish all of us, lonely people, had a cell phone with
Someone's voice on it that we loved.
But, people, you have your memories. Please call on all your good
Memories, for it will keep a smile on your face.
It will keep loneliness away.
Loneliness can be a personal thing if you let it.
We now know how to deal with loneliness,
For it's just the two of us, loneliness and me. But I can stop
Loneliness with all my memories, for we can face off anytime,
Loneliness and my memories. But hate can be the bigger picture.
There must be over seventy-two million people
In this country with hate in their hearts.
Some of us don't understand why we know we are alone.
That can bring on hate and loneliness, and we have no one
To talk with. But you do have all your memories in mind.
I write my story so we won't be alone, for I also need you,
My readers, as I hope you need me. It's all in the love of our
Memory. People, we need—NO, we must—pull together and stop all
This hate in life and in the world. We are all one people on
This earth, all colors of people, but the blood is red.
Readers, my days and my heart and soul belong to my wife,
All those. My soul is on the march, looking for my wife.
But I have spent time with you, my readers, over the years, to

Tell you what I know in life, that I, and only I, can see
What's coming down the road for us, people in this world.
Ever since I fell into that open grave at the age of ten,
My whole way of thinking has changed in life.
I feel that bad things are coming for this world.
I can see years ahead. Don't ask me how. I say to you, ask
Satan. Remember back when I was a very young boy, at the age
Of sixteen, and I built this old car from the junkyard.
Three months later, I was ready to test drive the car.
To this day, I feel that car drove me to the beach in
Maryland, where I met Regina, who was to be my wife in
The future of my life. That old car gave me the best gift of my
Life, my sweet wife, Regina, who I fell so deeply in love with.
The first day my eyes looked into her heart,
I could see it all—I could—at that age, all the love that was
In front of us. Yes, we were going to be the world's greatest
Lovers. Times were hard for us back in the day because we
Were black, but our love grew stronger over the years.
No one could stop this love we had for one another.
Seventy-eight years later, the love between us grew even stronger.
Sometimes the love we had even scares me, for I say, "How can
This be?" But I know the answer, because she was an angel.
She was my queen in life. She was one in a million. Need I say
More? Today I look toward the stars,
Hoping to see my wife among the stars. As long as there is
A star in the sky, I will keep looking up at nights.
And I will call out her name, "REGINA, REGINA, I love you, my
Darling." At times a star will blink. Could it be her, winking
At me? Could it not be? Who's to say? But to me, I like to think,
perhaps it was my wife telling me, "I am here, my darling."
It only hurts when there is no hope.
I now have her voice mail, along with her cell phone,
For I now have hope and love of a cell phone.
For now, she is in my pocket with a very warm feeling.
I open my last book on loneliness, but there is so much more
To life over and above loneliness. Loneliness comes to you

When you have given up in life or when you are all alone.
You don't need to be alone. As we talk about before,
Just call on your memory. We all have some good memory.
Memories are here for a reason, to give us peace of mind,
To give us hope, to tell us that we are not alone.
No one can take that from any of us. Memory belongs to each one
Of us. Remember that, my readers.
By the time you read this last story, my wife would have been
Gone well over two years. To me, it seems like yesterday. Her
Family in Maryland wants to give her a birthday party
For her seventy-seventh birthday at her favorite place,
the Fisherman's Inn in Maryland.
Her birth date is the twenty-ninth of May.
I had a lovely birthday cake made in her behalf.
On this cake was my words of love to you, Regina, my darling wife,
For I will love you throughout time.
Readers, I will most likely break down and cry at the party
Like a big baby, but I know my wife would understand.
After all, the party is for her. She has a very lovely family.
Today they are my family, for I love them all.
My wife once said to me, "My family is your family."
She also said, "Sometimes I think they love you more than
They love me." And then she would give me that lovely smile.
She was my beautiful angel in my life.
She was a gift from the gods to me. She was all my heart and
Soul. She was my full life.
There could never be two Reginas on this earth.
The Lord only made that Regina to care and love me in life.
She was what my heart was longing for in life.
I think I could have been in love with her at the age of ten.
I was too young to realize it. But she was then in my heart.
She would say to me, when she was the age of ten, sitting in a tree
In the backyard and wish for someone like
Me to come and take her away. She just wanted to be loved,
And, boy, did I love her from the top of her head to the bottom
Of her beautiful feet. She was a river of love to me,

Running through my heart. I was so in love. I could have walked
On air. She was a true artist of love. Her smile could
Turn a cold day into warmth. Even most women looked up to her.
All men loved her, but she belonged to me, and only me.
And she was proud of all her love for me,
For she was my woman in this lifetime.
She was all my hopes and dreams. Yes, she was the one person
That had it all in life. She had my love in her hands, as well
As my life, for life to me is only worth a penny without her
Love and her at my side in life.
At times, when we made love, in a moment in time, you felt like
A god, for her love came from deep down in her soul.
This was not your everyday sex. It was sex from the bottom
Of her soul. She was my angel, having sex with her husband.
For a moment I could fly. At that moment of sex, I was out of
My body. My heart ran hot. My body, before I knew it, was
Someplace else. She took over my mind and my soul.
I just let myself fly free. My body was her body for a few moments.
Then she looked up at me and said, "It's all right, darling."
To this day, my readers, this is why my soul went on a long march,
To find her after death, and to this day, my soul is still looking
For my dear wife. Readers, it's all about true love,
Real love, love that will carry you over a lifetime.
People love making the world go around. My wife was a very
Big part of this world. In fact, she was the queen of all women.
And I say that from the heart. She was real and lovely.
Her skin was the skin of an angel.
It was perfect, no defects on her body at all.
Her smile would light up a room. Yes, she was a special angel
On this earth, and she was given to me.
Every day was a special occasion for me with her at my side.
Memories, I am telling you about, my readers, memories.
This will help keep out loneliness for a while,
For we all have many memories. Readers, love is the greatest
Thing on earth today. There is nothing that can override love.
For love can bring on peace or wars. And over the years,

Love has been on both ends. My dear friends, we need love
Back in our everyday life. We must give a hand to one another.
You just may be amazed how nice a little smile can make
Your day a happy day for you. When comes a smile, there is no
Hate behind that smile. Smiling is a part of love,
Love for one another as good people on this old earth.
Remember, readers, give me love or give me death.
We must take love over all things on this earth,
For we somehow ran off love for now. Now there is hate and
Loneliness, but love, and love alone, is our keeper in life.
As human begging, we need love.
The love we had for one another stays on our mind.
How can I ever forget? I will never forget all the happy times
She had given me in life, all the laughs we had together,
All the living we'd done together,
The times we cried together, the times we made love.
At times, when we went for a walk, she would look back at me
And say, "Catch me if you can." Then we will make love.
I just smile to myself, and then my feet took off, and I
Ran her down. And, yes, we made love in the woods.
I don't think she really tried to run away very hard.
For a smiling face is a happy face. And we smile the
Rest of that day after making love. Yes, we were great lovers
Of the world. My wife was the classic lover, for she gave you
All that there was to give. She made you feel like a god.
You knew you were the only one in her life.
You had the right way to her heart,
And what a good feeling that could be to a living soul.
You then would become the happiest man on earth,
For you knew she was your woman in life.
Regina, my darling wife, my head keeps
        spinning around and around
In this old world, for even after death, my love for you still
Grows even stronger. I love you more today than I did yesterday.
My love keeps growing and growing. The pain in my heart is like
Fire throughout my body. But I need that pain. To me it is

The pain of love. I swear by all the stars in the sky, I will
Be with you one day soon, for your house is my house, wherever
You are, my darling. For I was made to love you throughout time,
As time will never end, nor will my love for you, my darling.
My mind is full of sweet memory.
Your lovely pictures on the walls are all over my living room,
And I just can't take my eyes off of you.
I love you, darling, all my days and nights, for they are so
Lonely. Reach out for me one more time in life, my darling, for
I wait for you.
Readers, there are no guide books in life, for life will never
Run a straight line. In other words, you are on your own.
You are the driver in your life.
Many times, I have gotten in my car and driven for hours
With no place in mind, just to take a ride and then find myself
Back at the house. And there is loneliness with a smile, saying,
"Where have you been? You know I will always be here for you.
You are never alone, for you have me in your life."
But, readers, I have what even loneliness can't take from me.
That is good memory. That's what most of
        my story is about, memories.
We had good times in the summertime when we would roll in the
Grass. We would laugh and kiss
And make love, then we would just walk and talk.
We would hold hands and smile.
Yes, we were very much in love, as you can see. There will never
Be a second chance of that kind of love for me on this earth.
You see, she was an angel that is now gone from this world,
For she waits for me in the next life, the life of peace
And happiness, where true love will never end. It will ride out
Time. And my wife and I will ride out time together,
For time is endless.
I will waltz with my wife through endless times, for we will move
Among the stars. We will spare our love throughout heaven.
For we are special, her an angel, me a boy from the dark side
OF life but found love in an angel that made me see the light.

Yes, we are special. There was only one like my wife.
There will never be another.
She filled my soul with her love till my heart felt the beat
Of her heart. It was then all over for me,
For I was now part of her body and soul.
Love for me took on another meaning in my life.
I was now the heart and soul of an angel, my wife. She was real.
My heart bleeds for her every day.
There are many ways you can love a woman,
But there is only one real way. Take her hands and look into
Her eyes and move into her heart and soul. She would then say,
I love you with all my heart, and then you both would feel
The power of real love. That's called one in a million.
When you lose a loved one, you will find out that time is like
A second in an hourglass.
Love is forever. It's like the wind; you can't see the wind,
But you can feel it. You can feel love. You can be with a
Person for years and feel love. You can't see love. One must
Feel it as the wind. I can say this because I had an angel.
My wife's voice was like a symphony, spreading love throughout
My soul. She could light up my body like a Christmas tree.
She gave me life and hope. Most of all, she gave me love,
Endless love that some people will never see or feel in life,
Because there was only one angel on earth that I know of,
And she is now gone. Oh, Lord, please help me. I need my wife
Back in my life, or take me to her.
Just give me five seconds with her. That's all I ask of you.
I have never asked you for anything in life.
I am so tired of being alone. Every day is like an open hole
In my soul. I just wander in life, looking for my other half.
All I do is think of my darling wife every minute of the day.
The nights are long and dark. My heart is like the night, dark.
The light has gone from my heart. All I can do is walk
With time. The little things she would do in life was unreal.
Just to reach out for me made my blood run hot. At times

My heart would jump a beat. Her love for
     me was as deep as an ocean.
I could dive to the bottom and drown in her love.
Lord, just give me back yesterday once more. But that will
Never happen. At times, when my wife would kiss me, she would
Blow into my ear, and I felt my feet was off the ground by a foot.
And she would look at me and smile. Was I really off the ground?
It felt so good. Today I am a lonely soul,
A lost soul, wandering through time on earth. I will never be the
Same man. A large part of me is now lost.
I do long for that Goodwill dresser drawer. I have forgotten about
That Goodwill dresser for years, but now it's back in my life.
But I have moved on in life. But I have no place to go.
I don't wish to go back in time, for my dear wife is gone.
Back in time, there were too many wars for a black man.
There are still hard times for us as a black person on this
Earth, and we lost most of them. I just want to move ahead.
In time, I just want to be with my wife. There is no other
Answer for me. Readers, I am asking for your help.
Your advice and opinion would mean a lot to me now,
For you have been with me for many years, from
Childbirth till the age of seventy-eight. Now I need your help.
It's not just about my wife and I today. My wife found her
Place in heaven. I am sure of that. She was an angel.
It's about me moving on. Which way will I go?
I have a debt to settle with the devil that I may lose.
Or should I reach for the stars, reach out for my wife?
I am so lonely within my heart. I can't cry anymore.
As I write about the ending of my wife's life, my pen in
My hand keeps going back in time, for her love is everywhere.
When death took my wife, it also took my life.
I would give my life today just to hear a whisper in my
Ear from my wife, REGINA. There is no other person on
Earth like my wife, REGINA, an angel you were in so many ways.
The look in my wife's eyes before she passed on, I will never forget.
Your lovely eyes said so much to me. I could read your mind.

You said, "Honey, I don't want to die. I don't want to leave you.
Will I ever come home? Please tell me, dear."
At first, I said, "Yes, dear, you will come home to me."
But in her eyes, I could see, she knew that was a lie.
As the days passed, she got worse, and she looked at me and smiled
And said, "You lie to me, dear. I won't be coming home (right)."
"Yes, dear, you are right." She said, "Dear, just stay with me.
I don't want to die alone." "I will be with you day and night, dear."
And I was with her day and night (ALL but one night).
I have no answer for that night. I said, "Dear, I'll be back early on."
She just smiled at me. I kissed her, and then I left.
Ten or eleven hours later, she died alone.
That is eating me up today. I wish I could die now.
I am so sorry, darling. Please forgive me.
All at once, I must face it alone. Your lovely smile is gone.
I sail alone on this big ocean. I must keep my balance, for
My heart and soul are pulled in two different directions.
There is no other woman on this earth like my Regina.
She could stop the rain and bring out the sun.
I know of no other woman with that kind of power
But the love and power of an angel. She understood my ups
And downs, and she would say to me, "Dear, it will be okay."
And at that point, I felt like a child, and I was happy.
She had that kind love over me. Today I feel like a lost soul
IN the center of the ocean on a skate broad or a pencil and
Scared to look down and dare to look back; my balance is not good.
As I said to you once before, where do I go from here?
I can't get off this pencil. I can't swim to shore.
The only place to go is down. Down for me would be the dark
Side of life. There must be another way in life for me.
God, where is that Goodwill dresser drawer?
I must open my eyes and get my life together.
Every day for me is like a blank page in a book.
This story is not about me but about my wife, who had passed
Away.
Readers, please forgive me at times, for I can't stop talking

About my dear wife, for she was my life. She was all my
Hopes and dreams. This book is all about loneliness and
Memories and how to deal with the two. But without my wife,
There would be no story to tell. So you see, I must keep her
In my story. Yes, I keep going back in time. That's who I am.
I am not your everyday person; that you should know by now.
In my mind, today I live in a world of fantasy,
For I have been to the gates of hell twice. I had Satan sit
On my chest. I have also bypassed death seven times in life.
Would you say I am your everyday GUY?
In your lifetime, you will never read another life story like
I am telling you today. I am eighty today. Feels like
I am forty-five, have the mind of a fifty-year-old man.
I have the WISDOM of a two-hundred-year-old person.
Does that sound like your next-door neighbor?
All because the hand that was put to me when I fell into
That open grave at midnight. Nothing's been the same for me
In life. So, my readers, this is not just another story book you
Are reading. This is the only one of its kind.
There are over a million books out there in this old world,
But there is only one ME.
For I don't know how to say goodbye to my readers or my
Wife, for my love will live on and on for my darling wife.
So permit me to jump from time to time in this story,
For life is not a guideline to a straight road.
For there are no straight roads in life.
There are hills and more hills.
Every day and night is different in your life.
But my life is very different than your life. Wonder why
I am a troubled man today. I wish I could just die. But for
Some reason, I can't. Will I live this life through time?
I hope not, for my soul now is running with time, trying
To reach my darling wife.
There is nothing for me today but heartaches.
My memories are like an eight-track tape, for I run it over and
Over, for I must, to keep away loneliness.

Please send that special train for me soon, my darling,
For my time here on earth looked like it will never end.
Satan wants to keep me around.
In my world, I feel like I am on the outside looking in.
For I live in the hot seat, and my mind keeps moving.
For I can't seem to rest, day or night. Every minute in
Time on this earth for me is a year.
Please, Lord, call on me, for I am here, waiting for the
Hand of my Lord. Lead me to my wife. Yes, I do believe now,
My Lord. My wife said to me, one day I would believe in the
Lord, and it took her death to put that into my heart.
I want to pay you back, my Lord, for all the times I failed you.
Here is my hand, reaching out to you. Please bring me home
To my wife. Only you can free me from the hand of Satan.
I feel I am on a journey to nowhere,
For I feel so alone. Unchain me, my Lord, from Satan and bring
Me home to my wife. People on earth may not believe me when I
Say the name of Satan, but that's okay, my Lord, for I know you
Understand. And you also know the storm is coming down on
Earth, for this earth has gotten too far out of hand,
And we just go on about our business, like everything is okay.
And that is far from the truth.
But time will reveal all here on this old earth,
Even if it takes the storm to rain down on us.
Readers, we know the right thing to do. Push hate and loneliness
Out from behind the wheel of that car, and run them out of
Our country, better yet out of this world.
Truly, love is our true friend in life and our hopes. We are
Happy when we are loved. Love is next to our Lord.
Hate is not one of our Lord, people. My heart is a festival of
Love. So if anyone is short on love, please call on me
For a lone, for my wife has given me the world of love.
I was, and I am, the great lover of all times.
WHY? Because I was married to an angel.
For it gets no better than to be married to an angel.
Readers, please forgive me if I make a mistake in my writing.

At my age today, my mind has lost a minute in time.
I don't mind an error in life, for life is never perfect.
Every day, any more is a special day in my heart, for I am still
Here with my friends. You, my readers, are my friends today in my
Book, for I love you, my readers. For I have never seen in life.
But one can only hope.
When a million years pass by, people will say, where did their
Love go? All you need to do is look up at any given night, and
You will still see our love running the galaxy.
For we will be walking in rhythm,
For we are endless-time lovers. We run with time. Love is so
Powerful. Love is everything. Love is endless in time.
Love is life after death, for love is endless.
It will never run out of time.
This is Regina and Ken. We feel we own the right to call love
Our very own. Many, many nights, I set home and cried, waiting to
Be with my wife once more, for love is unlimited. Real love
Has no end, for it will run with your soul, and your
Heart will keep your body warm. For it takes two to play,
And that is your heart and soul together in life, although
My soul is still on the hunt for my dear wife.
For my love will run with my soul throughout time, till the
Doors in heaven open up for him, and there stands my darling wife.
When we were very young, my wife for only a few months now
Said to me while we were walking, "Honey, do you love me, really
Love me? And do you know what love is all about?"
"Yes, dear, I do. And I do love you with all my heart."
She then said, "Is that it?" I was lost for words.
She then said, "Stop walking. Hold my hand and look into my eyes.
Just look into my eyes, dear." I then looked into her eyes, and
Tears started to run down my face. I felt so warm. My clothes
Where somewhat wet. I felt so good.
I could hear her say, "Are you okay, honey? Please don't stop loving
Me, dear. Please don't." She said, "I will
        always love you, my darling.
I will love you throughout time, my darling. Do you understand

Now what I am saying to you, my darling?"
Readers, we, black people, know all about love. We would die
For our women. We would step off the edge for our women.
They call that real love. You won't find that kind of love today.
That's called real love, not overnight love but true love,
One in a million today, our very own love story for over fifty
Years now, REGINA AND KEN. Honey, let's dance, for they
Are playing our song once more, the "TENNESSEE WALTZ."
Dance with me, my darling, all through the night. That's what I
Will say to her when we meet once more in the new life that's
Waiting for us, for we are two gold-plate winners on earth, as
We will be in heaven together.
My wife was always a shining star here on earth and in my heart.
Every day I could feel her love running through my body.
She would say over the tears, "Please don't die before me
And leave me behind, for I can't make it in life without
You and your love, I would kill myself," and she meant it.
And she received her wish. She left this earth before me. Now
I am the one with the broken heart. I am glad I was left behind,
For it would have been far too much for her alone.
For it's more than I can take at times, for I have you, my readers.
My wife would have been all alone. She would of not have you, my
Readers. I am the so-called writer, and I hate to write. Why?
Because I am a poor writer, but I don't lie. Every word in this
Book is the true story of our lives.
Readers, you and my books are the reason why I am still here
In one, and my mind is well for now.
For I must keep going back in time, for I ride with time.
I am saddled up, for time is like a shooting star, and I am ready
For the everlasting ride through time. I will hold on tight
To my darling wife, so saddle up, my dear, let's ride.
I feel the greatest life being when this life ends.
I am now in my eighties. They tell me, I look to be about
Fifty. On my good days, I feel like I am forty five.
On most of my off days, I am in my seventies.
My life has not been a good one or a basket of joy. If any

Thing, it's been like a hard structure, rooted in my soul,
Tortured, pained, and mentally anguished at times,
All out of my control. Come now, walk in my shoes.
Are you still willing? Life's been difficult for me as a
Black man. I face the white man every day of my life.
Then on top of that, I must fight the worst of all, the devil
Himself. I have had a tractor fall on me, bitten by
Just about anything you can think of, but I am still here.
Sometimes I walk around, like I am in the twilight zone, between
Life and death. Walk with me, my readers. Be strong with me,
But be scared also. You have good reason to be scared.
I, more or less, have tunneled my way through life the hard way.
I have given it my all and then some, maximum performance as
A black man and still came up short (roadblocks).
My pleasure and enjoyment and satisfaction is my wife, true
Love from the heart. She is my hopes and dreams. At the end
Of every day, I had her to come home to.
She was like a flower that never dies, a dream that only most
Men could only wish for.
To me she is one of God's angels that was sent to keep
Me on track. When I was a very young, black man, I would
Go off to myself and wish for a woman like I once had.
She came to me when I was heartbroken. At that time in my
Life, I was down on my luck. Many times, I was at the beach,
Walking alone, then along came this beautiful light, the
Light of my life. I knew, from that moment, she must be my wife.
She must be my woman. She must be my
        love. My heart was beating
So hard that I had chest pains.
I was at that point, just a little weak. Her eyes were
Like a star in the sky. I could see myself in her eyes.
Readers, I am getting near the end of our story.
The title of this book is for you, my readers, "How to Cope with
Loneliness." The key to loneliness is MEMORIES.
I have explained all of the key points to overrun loneliness.
My policy in life is to be true to myself and to you, my readers.

For there is no other like me in life, my readers.
For I am the last of whatever you may want to call it. You see,
I said it, not me as a person. For at times I don't really know
Who I am.
I am who I am. I love people—that is, most people. It seems like it's
Getting harder today to love one another.
The answer is in the heart, not the mind. We need to open up,
My readers, and reach out for one another. Open up your hearts
Just a little more in life.
There is room in this old world for all of us if we give one
Another a chance, for love comes in many ways. Love may come in
Many forms that the mind won't understand, but the heart will.
Always put your heart front and center, for you will never go
Wrong. There is a thin line between love and hate, but your
Heart will always take center court. The heart will never fail
You in life, only your mind can take you down the wrong road.
Readers, love will never disappear as long as you have a heart.
Today I am getting to be an old man, still can outthink most.
WHY? Because I live from the heart, not just the mind.
That Goodwill dresser drawer back in the day may have done me
Some good, for it gave me a warm heart. Perhaps you don't
Know anything about the Goodwill dresser drawer. It's in
The volume one and two. You need to read all three books to fully
Understand the true story of Regina and Ken, for we are the
True story in this book.
Readers, I had the good times of my life with the woman I loved.
Her name was REGINA L MURREY, my darling wife. I still long for
Those days. I remember everything about our love life,
For how could I ever forget she was an angel?
She was a rose in the garden of love, the star in my heart,
For she was every woman. She was my woman.
All women are first-class on this earth. They are number one.
But Regina was the queen of all women. She was an angel.
I could not ask for more in life for the queen that she was to me.
Why would a man be given all that sweet love in life then
All at once taken away from him? That is so unfair. What is the

Answer? We will never know that answer. But one day we will,
And I can't wait for it to come to me, and so does many others.
I just want peace in my heart today. I just want to sleep,
And I don't wish to wake up any day on this earth.
Satan has given us the shakedown. He'd taken our love from our
Hearts, and we are now in the back seat of his car.
We should be behind the wheel, not Satan.
Loneliness sits on the right of Satan in front.
When he, Satan, is finished with our souls, he then will give us
To loneliness. We must fight back, my readers. Just give a smile
Today and say hello. The feeling of love can come from just
A smile. I am not talking about true love now.
Just the feeling of a handshake and a smile
Can be love for one another. My days are numbered, readers. I
Just want to be sure that you are in the driver's seat
Before I leave this earth. All I can do is tell you what I know
Is going to happen. Look around; no one smiles anymore.
There are killings every day now in many cities. Even kids are
Being killed, and some of the kids are doing the killing.
What does that tell you, my readers? Is Satan on top, walking
Around? Love is the most powerful thing on earth.
It will take you out of the back seat to the wheel of that car
That Satan is driving. Come, come, my readers, let's take back our
Streets. It's time to pull together and yell out the word love.
Take back your world, for there is love deep down in your hearts.
We need not let evil come in and out of our hearts,
For we can fill our hearts and souls with love.
Reach out to a friend or a loved one, who you knew at one time
In life. Perhaps they would be glad to hear from you.
Make that phone call and say "hello," or "can we have lunch
Sometime?" And you will see how good that will make you feel.
For you may even smile, and that won't cost you nothing but a
Dime to make that phone call. It's called sweet love.
It tells someone that you care, that they are not alone
In this world today, that someone made a phone call
Just to say hello. Will you have lunch with me?

To me, my readers, Satan is very real. But to you, my readers,
That would be anyone with hate in their hearts.
Readers, love will keep us alive. It will keep us in the driver's
Seat. Yes, my readers, I will be leaving you in a short time,
For my time is very near. I can feel it in my heart.
What little heart I have left. I just want you to take back
Our planet the way it used to be, friendly.
Make smarter moves in life. Everybody is not your friend in life.
Some people are not what they seem to be in person.
Don't be fools by a person, well-dressed in a nice suit.
Look out for the red TIE. Also, look out for the white man with
White HAIR; he would be the man behind the wheel of this car
That's now running wild. You know I am right, my readers.
You may not like it, but you know it, the hard truth.
Readers, what I am saying, please don't be a follower or a fly
On the wall. Be a leader in life. Stand up for your rights and
For the people. Slow down, look around, and think, people, think.
You have your own mind. Most people are good at heart, but it
Only takes a few bad apples to rotten the tree, and these
People are mostly white people. Open your eyes and look around.
Who do you see climbing the Capitol building? White people.
When I fell in love, she was just a kid, but I was always an
Old man, even at the age of ten. But she was perfect, the perfect
Girl, and then became the perfect woman in my life. For we were
Meant for each other, even at the young age of fifteen. She
Belonged to me in life. I felt this in my heart, for she was the
Picture of true love and life for me.
She was my girl at that moment in life and the many years to
Follow. She was her Lord's gift to me in life.
She was perfect, true love in life for me.
Now that she is no longer with me in this life, somewhere out
There, she waited for me. She won't travel alone too much longer,
For I can feel my time is near. Every day to me is yesterday,
The day my love left this earth. In her last few days, I whispered
In her ear, and I said, "Take my heart with you in the next life,
And you will never be alone. For I will travel within your soul,

My darling." Since then, my readers, I'll be living the life of
A lonely man, just me and loneliness. I know all about loneliness
And what it can do to you after the love of a loved one.
But not even loneliness can take away my many years of good
Memories, sixty years of true love, real love, all in my heart for
Sixty years of her true love. Talk to me about loneliness,
For I have all the answers, memories.
Readers, some, over the years, may have called me crazy, but
I was crazy in love with an angel. I had the best of both worlds,
For she was heaven to me. Call me crazy if you want,
For she was heaven to me every minute of my life. If that's crazy,
Then I'll take it every minute of my life. Just to look at her, my
Soul lights up. My heart would beat even faster. She was my
Answer to life, my life. She was the woman that every man would
Dream of in life, and she belonged to me, and only me, for
We were lovers on this earth. And suddenly, she was gone. Just
Like a second in time, she was no more. Then my life was no more,
For I was just a shell of a man. Now I am lost in time.
But she left me with her memories and love within my heart and
Soul. My soul is still on that long walk, looking for my wife.
Life itself, my readers, is only a minute in time, for time itself
Is everlasting. Take it from me, for I have passed over from
One world to this world. I am glad that this happened, for in this
New world, I found the true love of my life, a young lady by
The name of Regina. She was waiting for me. After my long history
In the past life, I cross over to the new world and found
Most of my empty, waiting for me. Did they cross over with me,
Or are they part of this new world?
Most things never change. Bad things will always walk a day
Behind good. It's called mankind. For we are not perfect, but
We can do better, and we must.
Readers, the power of love is heaven here on earth. True love
Will never let you down. True love is the real deal of walking
The last mile with you in the dark and coming out at the
End in the light. Readers, there are many kinds of love, as I
Have mentioned to you a while back. But true love is once in

A lifetime, if you are lucky.
You will know it when true love reaches your heart,
For your heart and soul would give out the feeling that you
Have never ever had in your life.
For God then would have put love into your life. Enjoy it.
Give it your everlasting love. Give it your all, for this is
Your dream in life, a love from God.
For life is only a minute in time, but time is everlasting.
And your love will travel with time.
Readers, the way we were, we were MEMORY,
For we were lovers of time. We walked this earth with true love
In our hearts and soul. Yes, we were real lovers.
We walked in and out of time, for each day was another day of
True love. The test of time can be real love in your heart and
Soul. Readers, I keep saying I am ready to end my story now,
But the love of a woman for sixty years is so very hard to end.
Now, can you end the feeling of love over a lifetime?
I guess I could go on forever, for our love will travel with
Time forever, but I must find the end of my story soon.
Remember, my readers, MEMORY builds a bride between our minds
And our hearts, and that's good for the soul.
Yes, my soul. How far have it traveled, looking for my darling wife?
Let's wish it luck, my readers.
Readers, at times you can't hurry love, then at times love
Will come in a moment. For there is no time on love.
It will come to your heart at any given time, for love will set
The time and place. For you have nothing to do with it.
It will give you that special lady in your life.
Your goal is to treasure her for life. Give her all the respect
In life, for she is the queen in the life of a man.
Take it from me, for I go back long before your time.
I go back in the days where there were kings and queens.
And I was the king in my day. Now I am
        a man with a broken heart.
I lost the love of my life, for I lost my soul.
Back in the day, I was in and out of wars on horseback. Today

I am on my knees, asking God, "Bring me home to my wife."
What a difference a day makes but, in my case, a difference
Two worlds can make.
Sometimes I just want to get in my car, jump onto that
Superhighway, and run till I see my soul.
And we will ride together to the highway of heaven, where we
Hope to find my wife. Readers, I must get a hold of myself,
For I am a man of reason.
Readers, I am at the end of my story. I only hope I was of
Some help to you as I was to myself.
My story can run till the end of time, for there is no end to love.
I don't want to overplay my hand, for you may get tired of me,
And that I don't wish to happen. So I will stop the life of KEN
AND REGINA here. Have a lovely life, my readers, for you have
Been more than good to me over the years. For I don't think
I could have made it on my own. Just to have someone to
Talk to was a blessing in my life, for I hope you are a divine
Reader, for you have saved the day for me. Now I must go on alone.

So long, my friends,
Kenneth E Murrey.

ABOUT THE AUTHOR

Kenneth E. Murrey Sr. met his wife at the age of fifteen on the beach in Maryland and fell in love within minutes. They married two years later and were happily married for sixty years. His wife, Regina, passed away in August 2020.

> Regina was my queen in life, and she made every day a wonderful world with her at my side. I loved her with all of my heart and soul. I will love her until the end of my time; she was an angel on this earth to me.

www.ingramcontent.com/pod-product-compliance
Lightning Source LLC
Chambersburg PA
CBHW021120130726
47988CB00003B/1091